GUIDED MEDITATION

Tips to Find Your True Potential and Spiritual Connection in Life

(Mindfulness Meditation Techniques to Relieve Stress)

Cheryl Connolly

Published By Phil Dawson

Cheryl Connolly

All Rights Reserved

Guided Meditation: Tips to Find Your True Potential and Spiritual Connection in Life (Mindfulness Meditation Techniques to Relieve Stress)

ISBN 978-1-77485-265-1

All rights reserved. No part of this guide may be reproduced in any form without permission in writing from the publisher except in the case of brief quotations embodied in critical articles or reviews.

Legal & Disclaimer

The information contained in this book is not designed to replace or take the place of any form of medicine or professional medical advice. The information in this book has been provided for educational and entertainment purposes only.

The information contained in this book has been compiled from sources deemed reliable, and it is accurate to the best of the Author's knowledge; however, the Author cannot guarantee its accuracy and validity and cannot be held liable for any errors or omissions. Changes are periodically made to this book. You must consult your doctor or get professional medical advice before using any of the suggested remedies, techniques, or information in this book.

Upon using the information contained in this book, you agree to hold harmless the Author from and against any damages, costs, and expenses, including any legal fees potentially resulting from the application of any of the information provided by this guide. This disclaimer applies to any damages or injury caused by the use and application, whether directly or indirectly, of any advice or information presented, whether for breach of contract, tort, negligence, personal injury, criminal intent, or under any other cause of action.

You agree to accept all risks of using the information presented inside this book. You need to consult a professional medical practitioner in order to ensure you are both able and healthy enough to participate in this program.

Table of Contents

Introduction 1

Chapter 1: Beginning Your Day Right With Sunrise Mindfulness (20 Minutes) 3

Chapter 2: The Practice Of Meditation Can Improve Your Feeling Of Being Well 11

Chapter 3: Which To Do To 35

Chapter 4: Illustration Of Meditation Points 41

Chapter 5: The Constant Change" Meditation 64

Chapter 6: Moving Further 79

Chapter 7: Acceptance And Compromise 89

Chapter 8: Meditating Reduces Burnout And Stress. It Improves Your Focus, Memory, And Ability To Learn 99

Chapter 9: Exploring The Practice Of Meditation 105

Chapter 10: Anxiety Busting And Stress-Relief Meditation 113

Chapter 11: Hints For How To Study For The First Time 125

Chapter 12: Meditations With Guided Voice For Letting Go Of Fear 130

Chapter 13: The Light Warrior Meditation 149

Chapter 14: Dedicating Your Efforts..... 168

Chapter 15: Breathing For Relaxation .. 172

Conclusion 182

Introduction

This book will provide information about the different kinds of meditation, as well as methods to achieve it. We will go over the various types of meditation and then apply each one at a time in the hope of obtaining the desired outcome for each.

We will discuss the motives behind why we have to practice meditation, which is often is a tool that can be used to combat excessive stress levels and inability to relax. It is a common cause of stress and a inability to sleep. However, it is an exercise in your mind or exercise in your mind. It creates a feeling of wellbeing, and is now so beneficial in the busy and hectic world we live in It can be used to protect yourself against physical and mental polluting.

We will give you a step-by-step instruction for how to perform your first meditation session as novice and inspire you to keep going after you have felt you are seeing the effects beginning to take effects.

However If you're an experienced practicer of meditation, we'll offer suggestions on additional methods to do it, as well as items that you haven't ever heard of before.

Chapter 1: Beginning Your Day Right With Sunrise Mindfulness (20 Minutes)

The best thing about becoming more aware is that it offers numerous opportunities to rewire your mind. It is possible to do it as you start your day. This practice of meditation is ideal for those who practice it at the beginning of the day when you get up. You will be filled with vitality and energy to begin your day with a bang.

It's not just about increasing your energy. This practice will help you to become conscious. Therefore, continuing to practice these exercises of meditation will help you to learn more about you. A sense of awareness of your inner self can greatly affect your mental well-being. When you wake up to a stunning sunrise, you can begin to concentrate on yourself to gain awareness. When you master this you'll also be able to achieve peace of mind and peace of mind.

Make sure you get up early for this workout. It is important to be awake before sunrise to make the most of the impact of this workout. Find the perfect spot for you to relax. It is also possible to designate the outdoor space as your designated meditation area outside. It's a good idea to shut yourself off time from the world outside. Do not check your phone or your email. Spend this time completely alone, with yourself and in your own company.

Always begin by breathing... Take your attention on the breath... Visualize the fresh air of the morning which surrounds your... Imagine the air making its way into your body while your breath... Then observe it travel through your own body... You can see it take up residence in the lungs of your body... As you breathe imagine the air in your lungs gives your body life... Then you should begin feeling the complete force of your lung... Then observe the air flowing out through your lungs when the take a deep breath...

Take a deep breath... Take a deep breathe... Then breathe slowly...

You can feel your lungs expanding and shrink with each inhalation as well as exhalation...

Breathe in... Take a deep breathe... Then take a deep exhale...

Take a deep breath... Take a deep breathing... Then take a deep exhale...

As you look at the air around you make sure to be aware of your heart's beating... You can feel your heart beating in sync with your lung... Your lungs and your heart collaborate in such ways to breathe life to your...

Breathe in... Keep your breathe... Then breathe slowly...

Breathe in... Keep your breathing... Then take a deep exhale...

Take a deep breath... Keep your breathing... Then breathe slowly...

While you breathe, attempt to be aware of the activity of your heart... The heart is beats at a constant pace... That rhythm is in sync to the rhythm of your breath...

Feel your body vibrate every breathe... The body you are in is drawing energy from the environment... You can feel the energy of this positive source in your body...

Imagine this energy entering into your body... Visualize it through your mind's eyes and let it flow into the depths of your body... It will fill your entire body in vitality...

(Pause)

It is possible to begin feeling diverse feelings... They sensations are the body's reaction to the energy that you are taking in...

Breathe in... Take a deep breathe... Then take a deep exhale...

Breathe in... Take a deep breathe... Then take a deep exhale...

Breathe in... Keep your breathe... Then breathe slowly...

While you prepare your body and mind to focus, you must be aware of your presence... Be aware that you're only required to be moment... Be present in the present and now...

Every breath you take will take you closer to this moment and right now...

In this moment, you can bring your attention towards your breath... Allow the increase in energy allow you to concentrate on your breathing and remain in the present and here and now...

Focus your attention on your heart and the rhythm the heart runs... Make an effort to slow the pace... It is possible to do this by reducing you breathing...

Take a deep breath... Keep your breathe... Then take a deep exhale...

Breathe in... Keep your breathing... Then take a deep exhale...

Keep a steady pace with your breath... Then deliberately try to reducc it...

Take a deep breath... Take a deep breathing... Then take a deep exhale...

(Pause)

When you slow down your pace Try to be aware of the sensations that you are experiencing... What do you feel your body today? What are your muscles performing? How does your head react to the slowing of your heartbeat and breath? Try to experience those experiences... Take a moment to let each one of these sensations be registered within your brain...

You can leave your inner self and experience the sensations triggered by the environment around you... Are you able to sense the temperatures of your surroundings? What's your skin's reaction? Are you sweating, or is it cold?

As the sun is beginning to rise, you should feel the warmness... Do your best to feel the first sunrise sunlight... Develop your ears to be aware of your surroundings and... You should be alert to the sounds of the surrounding... Are you able to sense the world slowly rising up and begin to move about? You can also smell the freshness of the first day... Do you feel the freshness the new day is bringing?

The feelings should keep flowing... The sensations should continue to flow... receive an increasing amount of vitality... Breath gives you these benefits...

Breathe in... Take a deep breathe... Then take a deep exhale...

You are aware of the present and now... It's the early morning, and you are in a tranquil area... It is quiet and you are taking time to connect you with your self... To become more aware of what is going on inside and surrounding yourself...

Breathe in... Take a deep breathe... Then take a deep exhale...

Take a deep breath... Take a deep breathing... Then take a deep exhale...

Take a deep breath... Keep your breathe... Then breathe slowly...

(Pause)

Keep being present in the moment... Allow it to be a source of calm... Relax and let all these feelings relax your mind...

Get ready to begin your day... Get started to get yourself back... Keep going to let your flow of energy and energy... Then get your eyes open... Make an effort to move forward even though it's in the early hours... You're in a good position to face the numerous problems that life brings...

Chapter 2: The Practice Of Meditation Can Improve Your Feeling Of Being Well

The practice of meditation and meditation can help you to manage high blood pressure and stress as well as rest better and feel more calm as well as connected. It can increase the risk of coronary heart disease. It can also lower.

This hormone is that is referred to as adrenaline that increases your breathing rate and also increases the rate of your heart as well as blood pressure. This triggers us to take action and can be the right thing to do when you confront real danger or require to complete.

However, this "fight or fight" response can be detrimental to your body when it goes on excessively long or occurs all the time. Mindfulness meditation can help to manage stress in a healthier method.

Meditation can boost well-being and magnificence of our lives.

Recent research has shown promising findings regarding the effects of meditation on lower blood pressure.

Certain studies suggest that meditation physically alters the genius, and could assist:

Increased technology knowledge

The cognitive effects of the aging process

Reduce swelling

Support immune system

Reduce menopause symptoms

Controlling the brain's response to pain

Enhance sleep

Further research is required however, it is evident that the benefits of meditation on your body and the brain are obvious!

Find out the strategy that is most effective for you.

There are various types of meditation, such as:

It's as easy as sitting in a quiet place and focusing on your breathing. If the mind starts wandering (and it can!) Begin to slowly return it to its original place using your breath. Gradually increase the length of time you're in a position to focus.

Transcendental meditation is a technique which allows your mind to be focused on your inner thoughts, allowing them to wander in the midst of being aware of any other thoughts or feelings. It's usually a sitting position with your eyes shut for 20 minutes twice per day. Meditation with mindfulness can also involve an object of meditation, for example, the sound of the bell and chanting, or striking beads or gazing at an image. Prayer is also an intercession method.

Researchers believed that humans possess an index of happiness. Some people were born with a inclination towards happiness, while others showed the tendency to be more prone to sadness. The book from the Time declared that "neither the most appropriate choices or very good opportunities seem to be affecting people's happiness over the long term."

Today, we know that talent is constantly evolving and can be a catalyst for changes - that's not just new. Roplastik called.

There are a variety of scientific kinds of research that show the advantages of meditation. For instance, Compuware Corporation which is a major commercial software company, and employer of services in statistics technology located in Detroit, Michigan, supplied six 60-minute sessions for its employees for seven weeks. The participants identified a type of meditation that they called the love of mercy. Meditation that is gentle is an "technique employed to enhance the warmth of feelings and also to take care of yourself and other people." Participants were required to sit for at least 5 times per week during the week, for a period of 15-20 minutes.

The findings confirmed that production of this practice will increase with time through daily positive emotions, which will result in a broaderening of the non-public resources that are produced (eg extended thought as well as the motivation behind life social support, reduction in symptoms of illness). Then, these increase in non-public resources typically lower the level of satisfaction in life and reduce depression symptoms.

For the best benefits from meditation, you must practice it each and every time you sit down. Sean Achor suggests that even 2 minutes a day over 21 days could change your life. "In the time span of 2 minutes, which is based on two days consecutively it is possible to reprogram your brain, which will allow your abilities to be utilized with more confidence and with greater success."

It is believed that people who are emotionally energized manage their emotions and behavior better. People who are content and prosperous are more successful and productive. They also accomplish their goals more quickly.

Many studies on meditation have been conducted and have proven that it provides beneficial in many ways like physical elevation for your mind, body as well as your mental well-being.

In this article from The Huffington Post, Dr. on meditation. The process of learning through Elisa Adele and her stress-reducing advantages, according to Psychological Well Being, which she refers to as PWB, is comprised of the following components:

Self-acceptance: You're in a position of learning how to be generous with your self and be tolerant of others.

Self-confidence: You have an outlook on life that allows you to handle everything that comes to you, with strength and grace.

Personal Development: You'd like to explore new ideas and experience new things, grow and broaden your horizons.

Positive Relationship Positive relationships: Find people who love and care for you, and let go of people who don't wish to.

Life's purpose and mission If you want to go back to the world, or to remain out of your job to look after your children, there's an incentive to remain.

There is a number of people who doubt the value of meditation in order to reduce anxiety and boost healing properties, the most recent research obtained by faculty from the University of Massachusetts Medical School has proven that the opposite is true. It's really not as obscure after all.

"Neuroscientists have found that people who meditate shift their brains towards specific regions of the cortex. brain waves that occur in the frontal cortex that are prone to stress relax the rest of the frontal cortex. The mental shift that occurs is traumatic.

The effects of stress, mild Anxiety and Sadness "

A type of meditation known by the name of "Mindfulness Practice" is believed to be especially beneficial in terms of relieving anxiety and enhancing your living. Mindfulness is believed to be "the capacity to be in the present, not distracted and offers various wellbeing benefits". Buddhist teachings are over two thousand years old.

The trick, in addition to making decisions or reacting involves being aware of your present thoughts, feelings and body sensations, such as breathing. It is a great way to unleash your thoughts and let it go. Mindfulness Meditation is believed to be extremely effective against chronic skin irritation, pain, various fitness requirements that are attributed to stress and numerous ailments. If you live a balanced and healthy life, and have an a positive outlook on your life you lead, you're enhancing your health and wellbeing. This will aid in almost every fitness-related issue:

AdhdAddiction

Arthritis

Asthma

*blood pressure

Cancer

*depression

Energy

General general

U.K. Gauri Verma, MD of Gauri Verma, MD from the University of Bristol, says, "Evidence suggests that meditation can reduce stress and anxiety psychologically.

"There are general principles to applying meditation principles in positive states like depression and anxiety" the author said. "However the lack of research from population studies is looking at the advantages of any effective adaption."

Alongside the psychological and physical benefits , it is important to be aware of the spiritual benefits that result from a perfect meditation.Through you will be able to let go of anger and a general feeling of happiness.

Meditation doesn't require any specific equipment, and isn't difficult to master. It is a practice that can be done regardless of where you are and what you eat 15 minutes a day can be enough to put you in a specific routine. To reap the benefits, consider why you're not meditating already!

Dan Harris believes Mindfulness and meditation will lead to the next major health revolution for the public. I'm with him and am trying to I can think of a name that would take action on his prediction.

For this blog post, I've compiled an "Top Ten" list, or "meta-analysis" of of the most recent scientific research which support the various ways meditation and meditation can improve well-being at different levels and in various situations. Huh. I

Enhance brain performance

Encourage the development of creative thinking

Release tension

Fear of curtail

Expand compassion

The lower the risk of depression.

Reduce chronic pain

A low risk of heart attack or stroke

Aid in the recovery of cancer

Relief from pain after relief

1. Performance of the brain is improved

This journal Frontiers in Human Neuroscience was released to inform about 2014.

2. Encourage creativity

In 2014, Leiden University in the Netherlands discovered that positive techniques for meditation can stimulate creativity as defined by divergent versus convergent thinking even though nobody had ever been aware of it before. The research findings are published within Mindfulness Journal.

3. Stress is isolated

In 2012, Massachusetts General Hospital (MGH) and Boston University (BU) find out how an 8-week Meditation Education software led to astonishing results regarding the way Amygdala was able to respond to stresseven while no one was paying to it anymore. The findings of the study are published in Frontiers in Human Neuroscience.

4. Curtail Inquiry

A study conducted in 2014 of Johns Hopkins Medicine showed that thirty minutes of focused attention per day can raise the signs of anxiety, like depression. The study findings were published in the online journal JAMA Internal Medicine.

5. More compassion

Discover 2013's findings on Northeastern University College of Science and Harvard University, which examined the effects of mutual consent and focus on compassion. Researchers concluded that meditation enables people to feel empathy and support others who have was suffering, even when it was against the pressure of peers.

6. Reduce the chance of depression

A study from 2013 conducted in Belgian schools revealed that the it was possible for temperament to lower the risk of signs of depression among adolescents. The study found that mindfulness can reduce the symptoms of depression, and could even help prevent depression-like symptoms in the near future.

7. Reduce Chronic Pain

The month of February, 2015 with help from the American Pain Society, found that meditation can be an effective remedy for the pain in your neck that is chronic. Mes concluded that Mes discovered that meditation can have specific benefits for relieving the pain and also reducing it.

8. Lower risk of heart attack and stroke

In 2012 The American Heart Association stated that individuals who were practicing meditation through transcendental techniques were typically forty-eight per cent less likely to suffer coronary heart attacks stroke, stroke, or one of the causes mentioned above.

The practice of meditation has helped people lower their blood pressure, and also suggested that they reduce stress and anger. The more attention someone is given the better their results. The goal of attention is to reduce the variety of people dying from coronary strokes and heart attacks each year.

9. Assistance Cancer Recovery

Discovering this from the University of Missouri-Columbia in 2011 found that Mindfulness-Based stress Reduction (MBSR) refers to an approach to mindfulness coaching that focuses on yoga, meditation as well as physical and mental awareness about the condition of breast cancer survivors after they have been realized. It has been expanded.

10. Help with post-traumatic stress disorder

This Mindfulness Workout revealed in 2013 about the University of Michigan

Health System Attention, stretching and acceptance of thoughts and emotions aid people suffering from Combat-Traumatic Illness (PTSD) alleviate their symptoms. Of.

Mindfulness-based cognitive tests (MBCT) incorporate cognitive therapy and a meditative method of mindfulness that enhances awareness of your thoughts and emotions.

It's a busy world which is often hard to navigate, with a great amount of time to escape. We don't get even a single moment of peace throughout the day. Nor do we have the effort to spend time. We plan our days to avoid any time gaps occur, but we could be missing something important along the route.

Meditation is a way to get away from the world, bringing an array of extremely positive and amazing advantages. There's much more to the practice of meditation than what is apparent With a myriad of spiritual, physical, mentaland psychological advantages, everyone can reap.

Meditation eases anxiety and stress.

Anxiety and stress can trigger numerous issues, and can even shorten your life. There are some aspects of belief that are accepted as being true for anxiety and stress that when they are encased in the body, could result in illness and even disease. If you aren't able to discover a method to ease those layers of stress that build up in your electric field, these layers will continue to increase in size, creating numerous health issues. Regular meditation can be described as an escape for your mind. And it's more positive than the most powerful medicine that you can consume.

The psychological benefits of meditation are numerous.

Benefits of mindfulness can be broad such as increased creativity, reduced anxiety and stress, a reduction in anger, increased reminiscence, and even more peace and happiness. Regularly practicing meditation can also help in becoming a more effective problem-solver, and have an increased focus on your mind, which results in greater average productivity. Furthermore that it is psychologically beneficial, meditation increases awareness, increasing the likelihood of self-actualization and help with mood swings, increase confidence, boost self-acceptance, and empathy.

Meditation is a way to get to the heart of who you truly are.

It can be done anytime and anyplace; there is there is no special equipment required.

Meditation can help in removing dysfunctional intellectual and emotional layers.

In order to prevent depression or anxiety, sadness and addiction, meditation can do better, in the short as well as long-term, than drugs or alcohol to ease anxiety.

Meditation allows you to remain in the present moment

The emotions we experience often take over and keep us from moving forward forcing us to review and revisit the past, while fretting about the future. Meditation helps us stay in the present this is a beautiful and precious blessing. We often raise the burden of our emotions within our strengths fields which can cause us to weigh down. Meditation can help you let go of these emotional burdens, and often transform your life in a variety of ways.

Meditation can be the most effective way to get your relaxation of the mind and body.

If you think about how you can totally let go, then you will be able to step away even if for a moment, from the stresses of everyday life. You will be able to escape the annoyances, the obstacles as well as these inhibitions, as well as all the other annoyances of daily life in your practice of meditation.

Meditation gives us the rare chance to let loose our thoughts

"In Buddhism, in the Buddhist practice, the expression "meditation" is comparable to an expression similar to 'sport and' in America. It's a whole range of activities, not just one thing." Richard J., director of the Wisconsin Neuroscience Lab. Davidson, Ph.D., directed for the New York Times. Unique meditation techniques require a certain amount of intelligence.

It's incredibly difficult for a newbie to be able to sit for long periods of time and not think about anything , or be in the "empty brain". There are tools available such as an amateur meditation DVD or brain sensory scarf that can assist you to do this as you begin your journey. I

Meditation for concentration

As it can be difficult to focus and difficult, a beginner will be able to meditate for some minutes, and then do more work for longer durations.

In this type of structure it is possible to actually think about your mind and keep your focus on the object that is of your attention each time. Instead of pushing unrelated thoughts you simply let them drift away. As a result, your ability to focus is improved.

Meditation for mood

Mindfulness meditation helps the person to be aware of thoughts wandering around that are circulating across the head. It is not intended to connect thoughts or make them the ultimate decision, though everyone who is mentally aware is required to be aware.

Through Mindfulness Meditation it is possible to observe how you can be free of your thinking and emotions within the same way. As time passes, you will quickly become more aware of our natural habit of deciding to go on a trip as either good as good, bad or bad. Through the practice, an internal equilibrium is created.

In certain faculties of meditation students make use of a mixture of temperament and concentration. A lot of subjects are named after peace. This can be to an elevated or lesser extent, depending on the instructor.

Other methods of meditation

It involves thinking about bad situations and reimagining them in quality light, by remodeling them through compassion. Tai Chi Qigong, foot meditation are all shifting practices of meditation.

Benefits of meditation

If relaxation isn't the purpose in meditation, then it frequently occurs. Focusing on human behavior that is, transcendental meditation. According to Benson"the reaction in response to leisure has "an opposing, uncontrollable response". This is the reason sympathetic anxiety is not present in the system of effort. "

Research on relaxing responses have demonstrated the following benefits, which aren't permanent, to the nervous system:

Low blood pressure

Improve blood circulation

Heart rate is low

Sweating less

Slow rate of respiration

A little less concerned

Low levels of blood cortisol in the blood.

Feelings of wellbeing and happiness

Less Stress

Deep Rest

Researchers are currently investigating how regular meditation can provide long-term benefits. There are a lot of positive effects on the brain and the immune system for those who meditate. However, it is clear that the primary reason to meditate is not to earn. In the eyes of one Eastern philosopher, it may be said that meditation does not have an end in itself. It is a fact.

In Buddhist theory, the primary benefit of meditation is the release from the belief that it is not completely free of attachment to things like external instances or strong inner feelings. The liberated and "enlightened" practitioner is no longer unable to walk unnecessarily on experiences or desires and still maintains a steady mind and a sense of inner peace as a alternative.

How to Meditate: Easy Meditation for Beginners

This meditation practice is an excellent introduction to exercises.

Relax or lay down in a comfortable position. You could also purchase an incline chair or cushion.

Shut your eyes. We suggest making use of one of our cooling Eye Masks, or Restorative Eye pillows if they are bent towards the downwards.

Don't make any effort to control your breath. Simply breathe in a natural way.

Pay attention to the breath and learn how to move your body in every exhalation and inhalation. Be aware of the movement of your body when you breathe. Concentrate on your shoulders, chest, abdominal region and rib cage. In addition to controlling your pace or intensity pay attention to your breathing. If your mind wanders back on your breath.

Chapter 3: Which To Do To

Figure 2 Credits for Free

Training the Mind

The mind is the primary attire for meditation. However, in the meantime the mind is often disorganized, agitated and manipulated by the automatic patterning of the natural. The purpose of meditation is freeing your mind from confusion, but not to close it off or make it anesthetic.

The mind is not an individual entity, but rather a series of experiences and the recurrence of conscious experiences. Most of the time, these experiences are filled with anxiety and confusion.

Define Mindfulness and Attention

A few of the world's most well-known scientists Galileo discovered the rings of the planet Saturn by improvising the telescope that was powerful enough to investigate the vast skies. The telescope was not an easy one. The engineer meticulously designed it and built it with a steady hand, it was able to achieve satisfactory results. If we wish to step away out of the confines of what we are even in the most delicate of ways it is essential to be internally driven. One thing to note is that our attention span shouldn't be as short as the infant's but it must be filled with zeal and determination. This way, we can be able to see better results when the thoughts that we engage in hit the goal we have set.

What is meditation?

Fingers are pointed out to those who meditate. The people who step into the realm of mindfulness are thought to be selfish and with no respect for the lives of others. We cannot degrade the name of meditation as those who practice it seek to uncover their darker side and achieve more positive results from them. It's like someone who is aspiring to be a medical professional by putting in countless hours of training before entering the profession.

There are a lot of myths about meditation, particularly through the social aspects that we live in. The truth is that the practice isn't about limiting one's thoughts in a way. You shouldn't be constantly ruminating in the mind. Furthermore, it is not an option to solve your mind at a distance while being surrounded by confusion.

It is definitely beneficial to meditate, at least to a certain degree. There is a certain calm that can be felt. The release of stress and anxiety and breaking free from the chains of ego-centric egos that keep returning.

A Mastery That Makes US Free

As the story progresses we will learn how we can get rid of unwholesome thoughts, not by cutting them off at once, but rather by letting them dissolve into the realm of mindfulness. Therefore, in the future it is not that they take over us and instead, meditation helps to think different from the average person, but with a profoundly rooted way by transforming the inside.

To be truly free, we must not be a slave to ourselves, but be masters over ourselves. Meditation can help us liberate our minds from the restrictions we are faced with. This means we are in control of our lives instead of letting it be governed by the illusions and tricks created by our mind's turbulence and routines. It's not like leaving the boat to sail on the wind of the sea , but rather an alternative destination. The aim we'd like to achieve is to be free as well as to ourselves and the people in our vicinity.

In the Heart of Reality

Meditation is not a method of escaping the type of person we really are. In reality, it allows us to understand the person we really are and eliminate the mental apprehensions.

By observing and understanding the thoughts of our minds, we are able to begin to connect with a different set of emotions, joy and other positive traits.

The Liberation of the Monkey Mind

To accomplish this daunting job, we should focus in calming our minds. In the majority of cases our brains are similar to a monkey in a cage that, through his chains creates noises that beg to be released, but no action is forthcoming.

Once the initial thought is formed emotion, they also develop into behavioral and mood patterns which result in the character and habits.

It is possible that impulse-driven ideas will not yield good fruit as one could scatter seeds as farmer and expect to reap the fruits within bounds. We should therefore be the seed sower who is calculative and is aware of timing techniques and prepares the soil is of essentials prior to sowing. On the other hand, on the side of meditation it is true freedom comes from learning to master our own selves.

If we are able to consider that the main purpose of meditation is to open up new experiences in life. It's not the same as what it was before. So spending fifteen hours of reflection every day doesn't seem excessive.

Meditation's benefits be seen as a means of maximizing your efforts to achieve more joy. The lasting impressions from the pursuit are a profound way to be aware to the greatest extent the power we possess within our minds for wisdom, and also what we achieved. Therefore, the quest to accomplish this is an exciting and fulfilling trip.

Chapter 4: Illustration Of Meditation Points

For centuries monks as well as Buddhists have been able to achieve substantial tranquility. We often question how they managed to achieve it , and how they incorporate it into of their routine. In reality, it's lots of effort, and, more important it was a start at the beginning. Similar to other professional mediators, the beginner has to put in the effort and work up the ladder to become successful. The dedication and perseverance will help you progress from one stage from one state to the other until you reach your goal. The desire to be in the moment and the idea of progress must be discarded to achieve more effective outcomes. Your primary attention should be placed on the crucial element of your journey and not the final destination. This doesn't mean you establish goals only to go back to everything else. However, it suggests that being focused on goals can be helpful for a particular project however it can also be an enormous challenge in meditation. If you have an objective that you want to reach, you may be present, but the final destination may be somewhere else. The main goal of meditation is to bring both your mind and your brain to remain in the present. If your mind wanders, you'll be able to permit it to return. It is also impossible to get rid of your thoughts and be able to move on. Things like sitting can assist you relax in the present moment, and you will not be capable of moving.

Stress can trigger depression and anxiety. It can also make sufferers more susceptible to heart attacks and stroke. Studies have proven that people who meditate are less likely of strokes or heart attacks. It is because meditation significantly reduces anxiety. What can meditation do to alleviate anxiety? Meditation can have a physiological impact on the mind. When you meditate, there's an important change in the brain's activity. The change in brain activity will decrease the following factors: the rate of breathing, heartbeat the level of adrenaline as well as oxygen consumption levels, the amount of cortical as well as blood pressure. Different kinds of meditation may have positive physiological effects for the body. For example, guided meditation employs mental images that help to promote peace and relaxation. Transcendental meditation is, however typically uses repetition of a phrase or sounds to help clear their minds. In the end, mindfulness meditation is focused on the present moment and helps you to accept situations with no judgment. When you begin to meditate for anxiety, be aware that you must begin by taking fewer minutes and then increase your time as time passes by. It's simple to begin but you must begin by only one minute per day . Then, increase the frequency gradually until 10 minutes per day, or more.

When you begin breathing exercises, increase the length of time you exhale. It should be long and deep. It should also be more calm than normal. Now, concentrate on the way you exhale. Also, increase the length of your exhale than you normally do. After two sets of exercises, breathe and hold the breadth to the top as you exhale again. It can take 3 to 5 seconds or more depending on the way you can do it as you keep your attention on the breath and feel your heart beat in your chest. As you continue to hold your breath for longer the pulse will increase in volume. It is now time to practice simple techniques for meditation. While you are still holding your breath on top your breath be aware of and listen to the sensations that come from your heartbeat. We can identify the palm of your fingers by placing them over your heart. Look for a pulse on your wrist or throat using your fingertips , and then detect your heart's pulse. The pulse can be felt also in the neck, on the face or close to your chest.

However, remember that you must listen to the heartbeat in a physical way. When you are in constant contact with your heartbeat, take a break when you breathe. Heartbeats or your pulse will be able measure the duration of your inhale and exhale, which must be exactly the same. This can be described as the Basic Heart Rhythm meditation. As you work through these steps exercises, you'll experience the synchronicity between breath and heart. In the heart rhythm meditation the pulse is known as echo from the heartbeat. The reason for this is that the heartbeat is perceived as an inverse bit, whereas the pulse is only a single bit. Another method to make contact with your file is when you hold your palms with the palms facing upwards.

Take left hands and wrap them tightly around the right wrist. Repeat it until your pulse is felt. It is now possible to move your hands towards the chest. This will give you better connection with the pulse, and feel as if you're cradling your heart. This provides a higher point of touch with your pulse , while also calming your heart. These techniques can help you learn in meditation. It is important to understand and appreciate that managing anxiety in methods that are healthy can improve your living quality and eliminate anxiety out of the body. If something awful happens to you and you feel discomfort in your chest and your heart starts to beat fast and you feel it difficult to take a breath. These are the typical signs of anxiety that can be mistaken for an attack on the heart. Stress hormones are released as a result of emotions that trigger. They then affect brain regions which regulate the cardiovascular system, including high blood pressure, heart rate or blood flow.

In most instances anxiety is often associated with stress and depression. The scientists have concluded that anxiety and depression are a result of a shared biological process. This is because the majority of people suffering from anxiety will experience depression at some moment throughout their lives. This is not the case since the majority of people suffering from depression have some aspect of anxiety disorders. A long-term stress condition that is not addressed can result in one of these two or both. There is also an important connection with heart diseases and anxiety. For instance, those with excessive anxiety are often at an increased risk of having a heart attack as well as other cardiac issues. However, the problem is more evident in those who have an history of heart issues. The frequency and severity increases as increases the risk.

Each anxiety attack can have different effects upon the cardio system. Numerous theories have been proposed to explain the connection to the heart and nervous system as well as anxiety. Anxiety disorders usually alter the body's reaction to stress. This is because of the interplay of various hormone and physiological responses that allow people to flee from danger to be safe. An anxiety disorder can cause unintentional experiences that increase blood pressure and disrupt the rhythm of the heart, and can result in an attack on the heart. If the stress response is not functioning properly it can cause inflammation that results in damage to the blood vessel and lining. This creates a condition that is set for the development of coronary plague. People who suffer from anxiety have also been discovered to be deficient in omega 3 and fatty acids. Anxiety and depression also have negative effects on platelets, as they cause them to become more sticky and, in turn create an unneeded blood clot. Depression and anxiety also are connected regarding the diagnosis. For instance, if someone suffers from a heart condition and this causes them to experience level of anxiety. In addition, anxious individuals may also take on unhealthy habits in order to deal with the stress. A few of these unhealthy behaviors could be alcohol consumption smoking and drinking alcohol, both of which could increase the danger to their heart system. The negative effects of anxiety shouldn't be ignored at any point in time.

Meditation to reduce anxiety can help relax nerves and lessens the impact of anxiety. It's more of a method of control which keeps anxiety in control. Accepting the necessity of meditation is a way to prove that we appreciate ourselves and bodies and want to change and transform. Patients must also be aware that anxiety by itself is not the cause of depression or heart attacks. It may only be a contributing factor to certain situations. As we become aware of our responsibilities in regards for our health and mental wellbeing, it is important be aware of the contributions of experts and conduct more research into the issue. If one is experiencing signs that suggest a minor cardiac attack, this shouldn't be confused with the onset of anxiety. Be aware of your surroundings constantly, as there are emotional as well as psychological causes of anxiety. Be careful and use care, and don't be shy about expressing your feelings. If you're feeling uneasy to speak, you might consider performing some breathing exercises that are described in the book listed below. It is important to realize that you're not the only person dealing with this issue. It's a widespread issue that affects millions. It is treatable with positive mental attitude. You should also think of diverse ways to deal with anxiety to lead better health and a happier life. For anyone who has had anxiety issues, mediation is an essential part of your daily life. It should be a part of your daily routine and let your body, mind and spirit assist you in the journey. There is also an obligation to stay off of bad habits in your life that can harm our health and hurt our health.

Five key meditation points

Body Position

It is important to feel at ease and relaxed when you meditate. But, too much comfort can make it difficult to meditate, or get sleepy. If you'd prefer to sit on the ground, think about using a rug you can stretch your legs out and raise your hands. Make sure you're standing straight Your back should be straight and you should not stretch your neck. If you enjoy sitting on the couch, don't take a seat on a comfy sofa or chair. Choose an armchair or a study chair that is positioned upright without straining any muscles. This will make sure that you are relaxed enough to concentrate, but not so comfortable that you get lost in your thoughts. Your body posture can determine the extent to which you stay with meditation until the end or get distracted during the course of your meditation. While it is beneficial to sit in an the upright position during studying, meditation requires the same type of input. Following this, you are able to gradually begin breathing exercises.

Don't be concerned when your mind wanders or fails to focus immediately. Meditation is a process, therefore, interruptions are expected to occur at one point or another. The practice of sitting should not be limited to indoors. If you enjoy nature it is possible to go to a nature park or even within your own backyard. When you've set up your location and are ready, make sure to remain in a straight and in a comfortable standing in a straight and comfortable sitting. This is due to the fact that your entire body must feel and be aware of the exercises you're doing. It's fine to raise your heap upwards or downwards if you would like, but your back must be straight. Also, you will appreciate technology and download apps that will guide you in the proper body posture to meditate.

Be Present in the Moment and ward off negative thoughts

Be aware and attentive to the present moment. When you first begin your meditation exercises, you are instructed to master the art of working with various distractions. Most distractions are externalin nature, such as the smell, noise, or sounds. Others are internal like emotions, thoughts, and feelings. Always make sure to get rid of all distractions prior to starting the process of meditation. It is possible to enable during a time frame based on how long is set to allow for meditation. Letting go assists us in keeping our focus which is vital and essential. Without this type of intent however, distractions could distract us from the meditation process without our freedom or permission. If we are free of distractions, that we have set ourselves free from judgments, thoughts or any other issue that can distract us to the current moment. Certain mediators accomplish this by visualizing themselves as being a empty container. That is, they are empty inside, with no memories or a history of the past. In the beginning the person has an open mind and accepts any possibility. They are not in routines. When we meditate the mind does not waste hours pondering the past, and how awful it was or the unfairness of life. We concentrate on the present and how we can enjoy life and how we can enjoy ourselves and achieve more. We never overlook the opportunities that we are blessed with. We are able to accept the mistakes we have made in the past without regrets or playing blame games. In this moment, we wish to be content and will focus on aspects that will make us feel happy. It's like living an unremorseful life and enjoying what we have today. It's about valuing the present, without compromising on the future.

Sometimes, having negative thoughts isn't an easy task, but it can be accomplished when you know how. Take a look at the people around you, whether from your family or friends and even colleagues. Consider their attitudes and outlook on life. Are they optimistic in their opinions or negative, and could make you feel down? Are they encouraging of your approach to meditation to relieve anxiety? Based on this, you can create your own social circle to surround yourself those who can help you grow and who have your best interests in mind. A positive attitude can free you from feeling ashamed of the choices you do. It can also help you make the most of your mistakes, and allow you to move into the future more confident and more capable. You'll also be able to develop an effective way to deal with ease your anxiety and lead an uneasy life. Spread your positive energy throughout your social circle and assistothers to cope. In doing this, you'll be inspiring others and helping them become the most successful they are. Positive words will go a long way to helping people overcome their issues and also any other issue which affects them. In the home, you can be the positive role model and spread the message across the entire. The chances are that others will be inspired and want to become the same. Take charge of the emotions you experience because they have a direct effect on how you feel. Simple things shouldn't bother you. Don't follow the same pattern as others who react to situations. If you come across a situation which is likely to cause you to be anxious, breathe through and out, then say positive, positive words that make you believe that everything will be well. When you've done this, let that secure person you confide in and let them know what you're feeling. Inspire yourself to stay aware and accepting of things that you can't change. Keep yourself ready in the event of negative feedback, and accept the consequences with confidence. Prepare to let go of all them once they are all finished and over with. You'll come with a clearer and more peaceful mind.

Addressing issues as they arise to ensure you don't keep things that irritate you within your soul. So, all of to improve the quality for your wellbeing and a healthy living. Also, it helps you not put yourself in the position of blaming the happenings of events you have no control over.

Take note of the Heartbeat

The rate of heartbeat and pulse can indicate how anxious one is. Be aware of the speed or how slow your heart beats. This can be done employing your right hand to push your wrist. It is important to monitor this prior to starting your meditation. While you breathe in out, and let your mind relax a at a time, you should also observe the changes in your heart little. In general, when you feel the calm in your mind your heartbeat slows down to a normal speed. This is the reason it's appropriate to state that meditation is an effective treatment for anxiety and various mental ailments. It doesn't require specific equipment or tools. All it requires is a positive and open heart. Do the soothing music or calm surroundings calm your heart a bit? It's important to know this because not all people those who feel calm have an ebb and flow. While certain music styles be effective, others require peace and quiet. some prefer places where in which they can enjoy the natural beauty. If your pulse isn't rapid, don't get overly harsh on yourself. It could indicate that you're not in a relaxed state and you are still occupied with other matters. If this is the case it is possible to think about changing the settings or location, and then beginning with a new configuration. It's not illegal to begin again, as certain configurations could be more destructive more than other configurations. A reasonable pulse rate typically indicates that everything is operating in a normal manner.

Show a smoky Imagery

There is a vital meditation component that focuses upon settling on one object that is in focus. There are many objects can be focused on, including but aren't limited to candle flame or your breath or mantra as well as physical sensations. The majority of people utilize the breath to create excellent images in their mind. This allows them to maintain their focus and create an effective practice of meditation. Concentrating on something specific can help one get rid of all distractions and fully embrace the present moment. If you've had positive memories, they could also help you build the foundation of letting go of the negative thoughts. When you concentrate on the contemplative object, your mind will clear any distracting thoughts which can lead to stress and anxiety. The positive imagery creates joy and brings about positive emotions that create the state of relaxation. If you're satisfied with the images you are seeing it is likely that you will find yourself less distracted. You will more focused on the task at hand. There is no need to think that you need to stay with one picture. It is possible to alternate your images daily and the benefit of this is that a different image can trigger different memories, and which can lead to healing on all levels. Once you are accustomed to your meditation routine but, you'll find that you have a particular image you love. It is a good idea to make use of it more often.

Engage all the senses

Make sure that all your emotions are present throughout the process of meditation. The sense of smell may provide a sweet scent that brings back memories of the food you loved as a child. The rise of the rose may remind you of the most beautiful garden you've been to. The sense of vision may be present during the visualisation associated with the burning candle. When one is able to focus on the candle burning, one is able to eliminate thoughts of distractions and be more focused. Touch will be noticeable when you feel your pulse and securing your chest when you exhale and inhale. If all your senses are engaged and you are able to manage all the meditation practices fully and will experience the deep healing within you.

The decision to treat anxiety by meditation is made by the person who is concerned. It is due to the fact that it requires commitment and dedication. It shouldn't be made to happen, but the person who is being abused should be aware and understand that they're doing it for their own good. Young people are typically conscious of their heartbeats to the point that it can make certain people feel nervous. However, research has shown that as you get older, the awareness decreases.

Chapter 5: The Constant Change" Meditation

Everything around us is changing, always evolving. Think about the four months of spring, alternating between day and night , or the inexorable pace of the clock. When we suffer a wound in our souls due to an incident in the past We tend to believe that it will remain there for the rest of our lives. This is the case in the case of static creatures, but as being made by nature, we are bound by the universal laws of evolution.

All things are evolving both on a big and a smaller scale. On a larger scale, humans began their development many millions of years ago as the first organic cells began to form. On a smaller scale every one of us undergoes an individual evolution that begins from the time they were born until the time of their death. Actually, some beliefs and traditions suggest that our journey doesn't start or end when we die however that's not our sphere of interest at the moment.

What's important to know so that you can fully be able to appreciate the benefits of this method is that the way we perceive now will never be around forever, no matter how long we believe that it will. This is true for both positive and negative feelings with no any distinctions. I am sure that if you recently went through a tough time in the course of your existence, then you could think that you'll never recover. I hope this exercise can provide you with that additional confidence that it's possible and that you are on the road to happiness.

Let's get started!

Find a comfortable, calm and in a balanced and comfortable posture that is comfortable, relaxed and balanced. Allow yourself to fully be present with yourself and let your body and your mind settle down until they are at ease and comfortable.

Breathe in, relax...

Breathe out, relax...

Breathe in, relax...

Take a deep breath, be calm...

Breathe in and relax...

Breathe out, relax...

Breathe in and relax...

Take a deep breath, be calm...

Let your mind disengage itself from thoughts, and concentrate your attention to your breath. Breathe in a natural way and don't insist on a particular rhythm. Breathe in and let it let it go.

Take care, now, to shift your attention away from your breath to the space where you are.

Feel the energy and the atmosphere of this place throughout your being. Be aware of the sounds that are on the other side. Maybe there's a timer running, or perhaps there are cars whizzing by just outside your window. Whatever you think is good, make sure your eyes be focused on the outside.

Breathe in and relax...

Take a deep breath, be calm...

Breathe in, relax...

Take a deep breath, be calm...

Breathe in and relax...

Take a deep breath, be calm...

Breathe in, relax...

Breathe out, relax...

Bring your focus back to your breath. Relax and you will eventually arrive at a state of comfort and relaxation. Keep this relaxed state in which you can feel your body and mind totally relaxed, peaceful and at peace for a short time, and not letting your attention wander on your breathing.

Breathe in, relax...

Take a deep breath, be calm...

Breathe in, relax...

Take a deep breath, be calm...

Breathe in, relax...

Breathe out, relax...

Breathe in, relax...

Take a deep breath, be calm...

Breathe in and relax...

Take a deep breath, be calm...

Breathe in and relax...

Breathe out, relax...

Breathe in and relax...

Breathe out, relax...

Breathe in and relax...

Breathe out, relax...

When you've achieved the state of calm, we can start to shift our focus on the present. Let your mind naturally receding into the depths of your thoughts until you begin to see everything from a third-person view.

I'll give you a couple of minutes to complete that in case it takes some amount of time.

Breathe in and relax...

Take a deep breath, be calm...

Breathe in, relax...

Take a deep breath, be calm...

Breathe in and relax...

Take a deep breath, be calm...

Breathe in and relax...

Take a deep breath, be calm...

Breathe in and relax...

Breathe out, relax...

Breathe in, relax...

Breathe out, relax...

Breathe in and relax...

Breathe out, relax...

Breathe in and relax...

Breathe out, relax...

You can now be able to see yourself from the sky continue to follow the present, observing all that is happening both internally and externally. Every emotion that comes up as well as all the noises that are within the background: Everything is of equal importance and is worth paying attention to.

Breathe in and relax...

Breathe out, relax...

Breathe in and relax...

Breathe out, relax...

Breathe in and relax...

Breathe out, relax...

Breathe in, relax...

Breathe out, relax...

You will soon be able to see that everything that is brought to your focus will eventually leave your mental field and another thing enters it. It is important to note this and I'll allow you a few minutes to understand this, since it is the principle notion of the entire process.

Breathe in, relax...

Breathe out, relax...

Breathe in, relax...

Take a deep breath, be calm...

Breathe in and relax...

Take a deep breath, be calm...

Breathe in, relax...

Breathe out, relax...

The past was not here and now isn't anymore, and in the space it created, is now will be being introduced to fill the gap. Don't be averse to the continuous and steady evolution of what you're experiencing and seeing, as the most fundamental principle of the universe, and presenting itself to you in the most natural way.

Breathe in and relax...

Take a deep breath, be calm...

Breathe in and relax...

Breathe out, relax...

Breathe in and relax...

Take a deep breath, be calm...

Breathe in, relax...

Take a deep breath, be calm...

Breathe in, relax...

Breathe out, relax...

Breathe in, relax...

Take a deep breath, be calm...

Breathe in, relax...

Take a deep breath, be calm...

Breathe in, relax...

Breathe out, relax...

Similar to how noises come and go, in the same way that your thoughts continually change Your scars will heal and create space for new peace and beauty. All you have to do is give yourself some time and let the healing process happen, and not resist it with your mind.

There is no requirement to do anything except permitting the natural evolution process to unfold in its natural way. Being able to evolve means you're willing to let go of what is no longer serving you . When you be at a point where you are able to allow your wounds to heal, the it will be possible to allow new energy and positive energy.

Breathe in and relax...

Take a deep breath, be calm...

Breathe in, relax...

Breathe out, relax...

Breathe in and relax...

Breathe out, relax...

Breathe in, relax...

Take a deep breath, be calm...

Breathe in, relax...

Breathe out, relax...

Breathe in, relax...

Take a deep breath, be calm...

Breathe in and relax...

Take a deep breath, be calm...

Breathe in and relax...

Breathe out, relax...

Be aware of all that happens both inside and outside of your. It is helpful to identify everything by a specific name. For example, when you are experiencing a thought it is possible to say "thought" within your mind. This can help you see things from a third-person viewpoint, without having to judge what you feel.

Breathe in and relax...

Breathe out, relax...

Breathe in, relax...

Take a deep breath, be calm...

Breathe in, relax...

Take a deep breath, be calm...

Breathe in and relax...

Take a deep breath, be calm...

Breathe in, relax...

Breathe out, relax...

Breathe in, relax...

Breathe out, relax...

Breathe in, relax...

Take a deep breath, be calm...

Breathe in, relax...

Take a deep breath, be calm...

Be aware and labelling your thoughts the things you notice, since this reinforces the belief that everything will disappear and that change is the only thing that is constant. You are thinking but now you are hearing sounds, and now you're terrified, but now you've got confidence. It's a never-ending sequence of "things" and we are here to watch this amazing show unfolding our personal eyes.

Breathe in, relax...

Take a deep breath, be calm...

Breathe in and relax...

Take a deep breath, be calm...

Breathe in, relax...

Take a deep breath, be calm...

Breathe in and relax...

Take a deep breath, be calm...

Breathe in and relax...

Take a deep breath, be calm...

Breathe in, relax...

Take a deep breath, be calm...

Breathe in, relax...

Take a deep breath, be calm...

Breathe in and relax...

Breathe out, relax...

I'll give you a couple of minutes to concentrate on this before we reach the conclusion of our time.

Breathe in and relax...

Take a deep breath, be calm...

Breathe in and relax...

Take a deep breath, be calm...

Breathe in, relax...

Breathe out, relax...

Breathe in and relax...

Breathe out, relax...

Breathe in and relax...

Take a deep breath, be calm...

Breathe in, relax...

Breathe out, relax...

Breathe in and relax...

Take a deep breath, be calm...

Breathe in, relax...

Take a deep breath, be calm...

Breathe in, relax...

Take a deep breath, be calm...

Breathe in and relax...

Take a deep breath, be calm...

Breathe in, relax...

Take a deep breath, be calm...

Breathe in, relax...

Breathe out, relax...

Breathe in, relax...

Breathe out, relax...

Breathe in and relax...

Take a deep breath, be calm...

Breathe in and relax...

Breathe out, relax...

Breathe in and relax...

Breathe out, relax...

Then bring your focus back to your body, and start to feel your legs and arms again.

You can either close the fingers or open them to be in control of the space surrounding you.

Keep your eyes shut for a while and just enjoy the moment you're living. You've given yourself time to heal and that's a huge accomplishment.

Breathe in, relax...

Breathe out, relax...

Breathe in, relax...

Take a deep breath, be calm...

Breathe in and relax...

breathe out, and feel calm...Breathe in, feel calm...

Breathe out, relax...

Be aware of the surroundings surrounding you. Be aware of the sounds that surround you and temperatures of the space that you are in. Once you're ready, take your eyes off again.

Chapter 6: Moving Further

Mindfulness is the act of being aware in the body, mind as well as the whole world. When one practices mindfulness, they pay attention to the various aspects of their lives without judgement or trying to accomplish anything. It's the process of being free of any guilt, regrets or guilt from the past and returning back to the present. It also helps in getting rid of any goals or plans and planning for the future. In just for a moment, everything else is irrelevant--not your thoughts about all the embarrassing incidents you made as a child or the food you'd like to have in the future. It is then that you realise that you're only here for this moment, and your thoughts do generally not do anything to help in any way. If you were to sit down and wrote down what you're thinking on paper you'd laugh and realize how much junk is floating around in your head! A tiny brain, and no space to live or be. Thus we are brought to the art of living, being aware and present, gaining that eternal joy in this period of our breath.

In the modern age it appears that everything is in motion constantly. We have to manage many different tasks and playing different roles. Our brains spin turn to cope with what we're doing, and provide thoughts about the next step. While our brains are our trusted servant that contributes our survival, at times it may feel like all we are. When the things we consider and think about accumulate and become overwhelming, it's difficult to find joy and comfort within our daily lives. It is true that life is meant to be fully lived and enjoyable, but when our brains get overwhelmed and overwhelmed, it can be difficult to go from day to every day without being controlled our thoughts. This is why the practice of breathing and slowing down is vitally important. Being able to slow down and connect in the moment with your breath is the most beneficial way to take care of us and our lives. When you slow down, you discover that we are living breathe by breathing. There is a sense of connection to life when we realize this and living it.

The mind is capable of getting caught up in loops and patterns which can cause greater harm than benefits often. Mind patterns developed in our evolutionary process and could be helpful to survive by reminding us to consume water, eat food and to seek shelter or security. The brain patterns used to be useful, but they aren't helping in the same way as they constantly nudge us toward things aren't necessary to think about. There is no point in repeating the horrors of the past , just because there's no reason to think about the simple issues of the future. Now is the time to reset the brain and settle to be here right now. Your thoughts that recur in your head aren't necessary and should be removed from them. If we take a step back and observe what our mind is thinking while engaging in non-attachment, we become in a position to perceive everything for only what it is.

The act of labeling things in the process is an integral an aspect of the process. You can examine your mind and label objects that are passing by as an idea, a thought or an emotion, or even an obsession. The thoughts that go through our heads might appear as an aspect of our being, but in actual they're nothing more than a wandering brain pattern. Once you stop focusing on these patterns, you assist you eliminate lots of anxiety and stress out of your life. Detaching yourself is a process of meditation. Examine the factors that create stress or emotional reaction internally, and do not react to it. It's important to look at it as the situation it is, but don't be involved in any of the emotions associated with it. It's fine to be emotional; However, when that emotions begin to take over and causes problems in the way you conduct yourself and conduct your life, it's time to step back.

This concept of mindfulness could extend further beyond your mind. You can utilize meditation to notice and categorize things that happen in your body and through the breath. By observing any tensions or remaining sensations in the body, and then allowing them to be there. or observing it feels to breathe, and taking note of its natural movement through and out of your lung. Outside influences are something you can take advantage of to practice. It is about watching things move and disappear as well as listening to and allowing whatever you are experiencing to be present. Mindfulness-based practices can be employed to study and process many different issues.

By practicing mindfulness, you will be able to accept situations at a deeper level as the things they truly are. In accepting the events and happenings that occur in your thoughts as they occur, you release any deep emotional connection to them. Stress and worry will begin to fall off of an impact on your shoulders as they did previously and you'll be more relaxed. A practice of mindfulness meditation can be extremely beneficial in achieving an improved night's sleep. If you can learn to focus on all the noise around you, and focusing on your breathing, you can reduce any anxiety or stress and put yourself in an improved attitude. Being still and slowing down is what is expected of you. In the modern, hectic world, it can seem like something completely foreign. In a world where we are conditioned in our society to be constantly going and working, and then slowing down and resting is seen as lazy This is why it's no surprise that a slow, steady breathing doesn't come to us as easily as it ought to.

Consider how you live your life and live your day-to-day life. It is possible to keep a journal as an exercise. Write down what you do throughout the daytime, like getting up, stretching, walking your dog, working and so on. Think about the thoughts you are having while you go through your daily life. All thoughts of what you could be performing, the concerns all the worries and the scenarios. Consider if thoughts have any effect on your life at all? Are you stressed about money really help your situation? Are you worried over the security of a beloved one help them feel more secure? It doesn't help the situation. It is a normal aspect of being human to experience these thoughts, it is possible to ease themso that they're not releasing any negative energy.

If you worry or stress excessively the anxiety will carry you to sleep. The anxiety and stress can cause you to sleep in your beta brainwaves, trying to figure out a problem that you don't need to solve at this moment. A lot of the stuff that you are unable to sleep isn't even any solution. Your mind is so flooded by thoughts that they seem to never stop. To help you sleep better it is necessary to let go of the power that thoughts are able to exert over you. It is possible to let loose the control of your thoughts through becoming mindful.

Meditation on mindfulness isn't restricted to just helping sleep. it can be employed anytime of the day in a variety of situations. Imagine you are caught in traffic at the moment. You're at an indefinite halt on the freeway slowing down ever so little and at a snail's pace. It's driving you mad and you are barely moving at all and you can feel the tension in the air of the other motorists that are commuting along this route. Auto horns are sounding and brake lights are looming across miles. You're watching the clock keep running with the thoughts of missing work, while you are powerless and unable to do anything regarding the situation.

It is the place where a lot of stress and anxiety comes from and stress lies in the inability to alter the circumstances. This is a difficult place to be in. Although we aren't always in control of our surroundings however, we can take control of our own internal surroundings and emotions. When you are feeling stressed or frustration, when you feel like you're unable to take action or do anything, you should put your feet down and take a moment to take a deep breath.

Focus your eyes on one spot in this way. You can feel the inhalations and exhalations of air flowing through you and bringing you to life. Pay attention to anything around you by just acknowledging it. Note all the things that pass through your brain , and mark anything outside of you. It's about shifting your state of mind from one of agitation to one of relaxation. Mindfulness can aid in all situations and is especially helpful when you are trying to fall asleep.

The practice of mindfulness to sleeping can help you reach a an enlightened state. If you're suffering from insomnia this level of relaxation might have been difficult to achieve in the past. Now that you understand the reason behind your insomnia, you can take steps to improve the situation. You can practice the different meditations that are in this book, and attempt to let the mental clutter go away in this process. At first you'll want to make everything better but you might experience discontent when things do not change. Instead, try accepting and allowing what is present to exist. Through the process of observation, without attachment, you'll be able to experience this state of mindfulness. As you practice you will discover it much easier and simpler to observe, but also let these thoughts go completely. You may one day be able to experience the joy of not letting thoughts disturb you, while being at peace.

You are now in the right direction on your way to easing your sleep. Thank you for taking this amazing step towards something that is extremely beneficial and effective. You can be sure that you'll find relief and a greater sense of peace and tranquility in the near future. Continue to keep doing your meditations, and let yourself be open and accepting. Then, relax and take a deep breath and then continue to dive further and deeper into these exercises.

Chapter 7: Acceptance And Compromise

One of the most important aspects of learning to relax through mediation is accepting and compromising. It's a bit, similar to the way that commitment and acceptance aid in therapy, but there are additional aspects to consider here. In this article, we'll explore acceptance, compromise and how it could play part in the overall success of your life. We'll also discuss how accepting certain aspects of yourself, and any other distractions can assist you compromise and conquer the fears that come with life.

Anxiety and Mind

Anxiety is present at times to help keep us in a safe place. Stress is necessary to push us in an direction, or to increase the heart rate and the breathing more rapid. However, the issue with stress is that taking too much of something that is normal for you, is not.

Anxiety helps keep us safe. Stress helps to keep us on track But the issue is that it's automatic, and operates on autopilot. And sometimes it does work, but sometimes it isn't.

After a day with lots in stress shouldn't have to be constantly thinking about stress. It's not a good idea to be constantly stressed. When you are able to recognize the moments when you're stressed and overwhelmed, you'll be in a position to improve your response to stress and make it more comfortable. The body might think that there is stress occurring constantly, even though you're doing nothing. This isn't healthy and it could cause you to feel sick.

Relax your body as stress can alter blood pressure, which can cause health issues. However, with the proper relaxation techniques, you will be able to tackle anxiety and get it under control.

Accepting

It's not possible to eliminate anxiety, or turn off your anxiety. You must learn you can harness this power. It is a powerful force once you are able to calm it. by practicing meditation, specifically guided meditation, you'll be able to reduce this, and while it may be present, you're strengthening your brain to the point that instead of reacting with a fighting or flight mode you're embracing it as an integral part of who you are.

Since here's the fact of the matter: you won't magically make stress or anxiety disappear. The burden of expenses or taking care of children or working all of it is there regardless of whether you want the idea or not. The practice of mindfulness can increase and strengthen the brain to withstand the various anxieties of everyday life. You should, as a result take the time to accept anxiety as it is and then you can reduce the volume on these thoughts.

This is why, in meditation whenever these thoughts pop up, you try accepting them, and do not fight it. If you are sitting in the floor in a calm place and do mindfulness, it is likely that the negative thoughts will begin be surfacing. This happens often, and you may find yourself feeling anxious again. If you take the time to realize that it's happening and accepting them and accepting it, you'll feel much better when you get there, and be able keep anxiety at lower levels.

Changes in this will not be easy and will not happen in a single day. When you meditate, you could notice the effects of greater relaxation instantly however, overcoming the habit of feeling overwhelmed or stressed or believing that you have to be always stressed may be more difficult than you think. That's the main reason people experience when struggling with anxiety. Knowing that you have to make small changes is an important aspect of changing the way you feel and adjusting the various aspects of it too.

Compromise

You've experienced the anxiety that you feel, you've accepted it will exist However, how do you handle the risk of this. When these feelings come they might stay and then disappear. If you are trying to control this through meditation, remember that it won't remain for long. You don't need to live with this.

What you should do when you're stressed, is be present in the moment, and not having the need to ignore any thoughts or feelings for the reason. There's no reason to be uneasy after a while and you should accept it and, if it doesn't disappear in a flash, consider a compromise and realize that they're not going to disappear immediately. Be flexible, trustworthy, and open. You should stay until you be able to accept that you don't really have to use to have them. You must be prepared to accept that they'll leave once they're done.

While you're meditating do not think that your thoughts will be gone by force.

Meditation allows you to look at the thoughts, accept that they are there, and you may need to accept that they will not go away. They might stay even though I understand that it's extremely annoying and extremely frustrating, pushing away like they're nothing and attempting to force them to go away does not make sense. It's just not working. It will only cause you to feel more miserable as you age and you'll only be able to resent this and your self even more. Therefore, in the interest of your own health and well-being, don't force these things away. Instead, make it a point to compromise.

Compromise can resolve conflicts of all kinds

When it comes to disputes of all kinds or conflicts, whether it's an argument with your mind or with a person it is a good idea to compromise an integral part of it. Compromising can help balance the views of both parties and result in an exchange of demands and requirements, basically reaching a middle. This is essential for any healthy relationship, because without compromise, it's nearly impossible for a compromise to occur and you're not going to feel comfortable about it.

What is the role of this in meditation? If you're not willing to confront and comprehend the negative thoughts you have, and learn to accept them and to compromise to reach an agreement with them and accept them as a part of your life, you'll never get better!

This is the cause-and-effect mindset that many people engage in. We speak about the concept of cause and effect in order to find a way to improve your life. in case you wish to improve your life it is your responsibility to make a decision on the subject. This is also true of meditation as well. If you're ready to transform your thoughts of meditation into something that is more pleasant, relaxing, and more able to be felt and experienced, then you'll have more charge of your personal wellbeing, health, and happiness.

Let's consider this as an illustration. You're contemplating to ease stress, and you're finding that regardless of whatever you do you're not at ease, or perhaps you're constantly thinking about it. So, are you embracing this stressful feeling? Are you trying to find a place at the middle of the road to comprehend the reasons it's happening and what it is doing to stop you from feeling stressed?

Most likely, you don't know, and this is the thing you're doing wrong.

If you're confronted with negative thoughts, feelings , and similar thoughts, feelings, and so on, the most effective way to deal with them is to ensure that you're ready to accept them for the way they're. Take a look at them and accept them.

It doesn't mean you have to allow them to be a part of your life forever. Instead, you should work to compromise and ensure that you're working through all these aspects and attempting to comprehend.

The ability to accept your feelings is an essential part of the process of resolving conflicts. This doesn't mean you must offer them a free invitation to remain there throughout your life. Here's the reality If you'd like the feelings to not dominate your life and you wish to know how to be mindful of them, so that you can build a happier and healthier outlook Then, yes, you must learn to be accepting of them.

Understanding both sides and understanding that emotions are present is an important aspect of compromise. You could, if you allow them in and admit that they're to be here, examine the issues and discover what they are and the reason for all this stress. What are you lacking to do better at managing stress? Do you require to be more proactive about negative thoughts? If yes, then take action.

If it's anxiety that is manifesting take a look at what's creating your anxiety. Consider the triggers that are causing it to understand and build these, and reflect on these. Learn, and be able to accept them. Eventually, you'll see that it's better to compromise and be acc3pt instead of pretending they're not there. Making sure you are savvy in how you manage your anxiety and learning to accept, as well as compromise will play an important aspect in your capacity to succeed in this.

That's the lesson you need to be learning from this. Be open to experiencing the things you must encounter and know why you do things in the way you do. Acceptance is a key factor in how you deal with situations, no matter those you think about or stress manifesting or anxiety. Being capable of showing empathy for theseand gaining an understanding of what triggers them , will enable you to identify your triggers and develop a greater understanding of what triggers the behavior you experience and, over time you'll be more content by the outcome and better off in the end.

Chapter 8: Meditating Reduces Burnout And Stress. It Improves Your Focus, Memory, And Ability To Learn

Meditation is frequently regarded as a way to lower stress levels and also improving the overall health of a person. Additionally, this type of exercise is believed by many to bring harmony between the body and soul. If you've never tried this kind of workout prior to this article, it will help you start your adventure so that, in the end, you will become able to discover your true self.

Meditation Techniques for Curbing Depression

The practice of meditation can help one to manage and relax their mind. In general, the mind of a human is often very powerful, and it is a fact that no person can ignore the fact that our thoughts are the primary factor in determining our moods, emotions, and moods. If a person is afflicted by anxiety, depression or depression or stress, a variety of negative thoughts are likely to be a part of their mind. The more negative thoughts cloud an individual's mind the worse he or she feels. The long-term effects can cause an individual to be more susceptible to the chronic depressive disorder.

Stress is now proving to be a common feature of our lives there is more important to reduce its negative effects through practicing meditation. This can to induce a state that is a deep relaxation or relaxation which is usually the complete opposite of the stress response. In essence, when you sit down to meditate and train your mind to focus only on positive aspects of your life. Beginning your day with a routine of meditation can aid in gaining focus and clarity, and in the end, you'll be able to put your mind at peace. Here are some examples of various ways to meditate:

* Yoga Meditation:-

This type of meditation is generally regarded by the majority of people as a sequence of exercises that are done when a person is sitting on a mat for an organized class. One of the most important aspects about this kind of workout is that one is not required to alter his or her routine because yoga can teach the individual to alter their routine and manage the level of awareness and focus an individual brings to their exercises.

* Buddhist Meditation:

Buddhist meditation usually aims to make a person more detached which allows the person to cope with physical pains and heavy emotions like fear and anger without suffering. The loss of equanimity is because of the desire of an individual to get rid of the negative or to hold on to the present. If someone is detached the issues usually go away quickly.

* Soham Meditation:-

According to certain religions according to some religions, when you do the soham meditation you are in fact recalling God. That means that with every breaths you take, you are praying or worshipping God. While doing this kind of yoga exercise, focusing on your breathing can help in gaining focus and clarity.

3. Third Eye Meditation:

"Be aware, remain in silence while letting the illumination reveal itself" is the usual tack employed in this type of meditation. The third eye is about allowing a person to open their consciousness to the light , so that at the end the the truth will be discovered. In general, when a person begins to see the truth or the truth about this universe, it becomes apparent that he or she had been fooled by external influences to believe that they are piece of the Universe. Third eye meditation can help people to open their his third eye, by which one will be in a position to see the many amazing things in the universe.

* Vipassana Meditation:-

Similar to other meditation methods, the principle behind this meditation technique is to achieve without hassle the ability to see the world and the people around as they actually are and without judgement. Vipassana meditation teaches people how to achieve transformation through observation. It is the practice of observing specifically observe the connection between the body and the mind. While practicing vipassana the observation of oneself is usually demanded.

Chapter 9: Exploring The Practice Of Meditation

There's nothing more you require to relax than an open mind. However, here are some guidelines that will help you get exercising. If you feel annoyed or unhappy with your work, return here to the section. Meditation is for everyone. In yoga, we frequently hear people saying, "Oh, I can't practice yoga, I'm not able to do it because of my inflexibility." This argument is confusing to me since people believe that the result of the exercise (flexibility) should be considered a requirement to even try it, which is not the case. In the case of meditation, the same principle applies. If you're a person who thrives in business and is described as anxious tired, exhausted or anxious If you're like that, the practice of meditation not for you. It's an ideal choice for you. Meditation helps people with their thoughts and lives to discover peace and space. It also helps you realize that the self-concepts you have about yourself ("I'm overwhelmed") can be just thoughts, so you don't have to accept these thoughts for long.

It's your Time. A few minutes of quiet is more effective than nothing at all. It can be difficult to prioritize something that seems to be not "productive" initially. However, the truth is that meditation is extremely productive, possibly among the most efficient things you can do in five to 10 minutes. Make time for it. There's no need for to have a number. Make sure to schedule your next workout on the calendar or schedule the alarm on your mobile. Be consistent and stick to it--I'm sure that in the course of your day, you will take 5-10 hours...

SCREENING THE SPACE

It is possible to meditate wherever you want: on the train, on the air or conference room, or in the lobby of a hotel. Try to reduce distractions. This can be beneficial, especially at the beginning. There is no need for a specific seat or cushion, however you do want to feel comfortable physically. A lot of noise can make focusing at first easier, so choose the most tranquil spot. It is also possible to listen with your headphones or the speakers to calm ambient music that blocks out background sound. Find a spot in your home where you enjoy some peace and comfort and make it your personal meditation spot.

Unplugging

Set your phone to plane mode (unless you are using it for headphones to listen to music In which case all notifications should be turned off). Shut down the computer or put it into sleep mode. Turn off any alarms which may disturb you. This moment is usually accompanied by challenges beyond our control, that may be overwhelming, however they are essential to face. The digital world is an aspect that is completely out of our control So unplug and put electronic devices away before settling into.

GETTING RELAXED

Find an area that is comfortable where you are. You could sit on benches, a chair or even a bench at the foot of the stairs. Try to locate a place in which, after a couple of minutes you'll not get exhausted and your legs won't be able to fall asleep. If you're at an area that is public, make sure you position yourself so that you aren't distracted, to ensure you're not getting in the way. If for some reason, you're not sure that sitting will be your ideal choice lying on your back could be a good option, but you run the chance of getting sleepy. The ideal situation is to like to relax, but not so relaxed that you'll drift off.

All you have to do is to try. Be aware of this when you start your practice that meditation is not a way to "fail." It's true that you might be having trouble however, you have experienced practitioners who are who are struggling. Take it easy. There are no rules to meditation therefore don't get too strict about the process. Even meditation is beneficial for thirty minutes.

Make sure you take the amount of time each practice demands and try to concentrate your attention in the present. In time, you'll be able to find the rhythm and method that you can use. You'll reap many benefits from meditation as long as you're willing to try.

How do I know if Meditation Is Effective?

Keep in mind that meditation is designed to help you gain a clear understanding of the present. Once you have done this you'll begin to view your emotions as opinionsand not reality, and you'll start to see a gap between the stressors and your responses. With these techniques it is possible to discover an endless variety of ways that meditation can assist you in your everyday life. When you start to notice that you're taking longer breaths throughout the day or you're letting thoughts flow instead of recording them, or feeling more at ease, relaxed or sleeping better You'll be able to tell that meditation can be effective.

How to make this book Work for You

It's your diary designed to assist you in your to practice meditation. Meditation practices are distinct from one another, and you don't have to follow a particular sequence. Pick the practices that you enjoy the most and repeat as many times as you'd enjoy. Start by experimenting with the new method for each practice until you find the one that works for you. Take the meditations that follow as your first steps in a fascinating and open-ended path of self-discovery. They're designed to ease stress, encourage relaxation, and improve sleeping quality however, you may experience more dramatic shifts. Do not let them go away. Continue on your way. Continue exploring.

Stretch Out Yourself and Do the

The cover of the book varies in length. Some cover five minutes long, while others are 25 minutes. I would encourage everyone to give them a try. Simply by going through them, you'll not be able to determine which ones are most effectively for your needs. You must practice these.

Begin with shorter exercises and then get going. When you feel more comfortable, you can try the techniques for longer and longer.

Accept Your Displeasure

As you work You'll probably experience some irritability or unease at times (maybe even daily). Keep in mind that emotions are created by your mind. Take them in allow them to go. If they're that strong, you are unable to return to your meditation, then taking a step off is fine. Do not let this become the final time that you've tried meditation. And do not keep your anger around. Take them off, reflect, try another thing, review the principles here, and then start over. In addition, those who have the most experience confront emotional and psychological resistance as I explained earlier. This kind of force is normal. It is only acceptable as it is.

Keep the journey going!

I am adamant about the power of meditation that is not evident at this point. I am happy to share the following practices and I truly believe that you will find these activities beneficial. If you're new to meditation, you should often refer back to this chapter to receive encouragement and to remind yourself that to stay on path. Keep in mind that you're going on a journey where you will encounter new experiences and discover yourself again, seeking out more space to relax, clarity, and clarity which is why resting is the best result. This trip is definitely worth it.

Chapter 10: Anxiety Busting And Stress-Relief Meditation

You should be getting basics at this point. Prepare to take your first steps into higher levels on your meditation journey by conquering anxiety. The anxiety builds up and cause your mind to experience to a tense state. Then you experience an unexpected anxiety attack at the time you least expected it. This practice of meditation will assist in the event that your anxiety suddenly comes suddenly. You can reduce your anxiety if you practice a pause and meditate on mindfulness. In the end, as a result of this activity, you'll experience a great relief from stressful emotions.

This meditation practice should let you relax. Let yourself enjoy just a few minutes of solitude time to get rid of the worries and stressors that are trying to burden you. Relax and let your mindfulness do wonders for your body and mind. Just a short amount of time during this meditation practice will leave you feeling calm and refreshed.

It is a good idea to try this exercise whenever stress and anxiety begin and escalate to an uncontrollable degree. When you begin to feel anxiety and stress rise, to a place that is quiet in which you are able to be completely alone. You must ensure that the location gives you the space and privacy you require. You definitely don't want be disturbed while going through this.

Settle into a comfortable position. Avoid straining any area in your body. Be sure that your muscles aren't tight as they are when you do this. Place your arms at your side or put the hands of your lap. Start by closing your eyes.

Close your eyes ... First thing that you must do is be conscious of the necessity of stopping... You have to stop... You have to stop whatever that you had been taking care of... You must stop any thoughts from occupying your mind...

Then, focus in your breathing...

Take a deep breath... Keep your breathe... Then breathe slowly...

Breathe in... Take a deep breathing... Then breathe slowly...

Take a deep breath... Take a deep breathe... Then take a deep exhale...

When you exhale and inhale take a moment to notice the sensations you experience as you breathe... Let the sensations to softly coax them to surround your... Feel their influence... Feel the weight that's trying to weigh you down... It must be some tension in your shoulders and head...

While you remain focused on your breathing Allow these feelings to overflow your entire body... These sensations will be clear within your awareness... Then you are able to sense the weight of the weight that you are carrying around your shoulders and your head... The muscles in your body are beginning to become very tense... and other parts of your body may begin to feel tension as well... Take note of the rumbling inside your stomach... This is common signs of a body full of stress... Simply bring your attention into these unpleasant sensations...

After that, return in your breath... Concentrate on the breath... Allow it to be your only attention right now...

Breathe in... Take a deep breathing... Then take a deep exhale...

Breathe in... Take a deep breathe... Then exhale slowly.

Breathe in... Take a deep breathing... Then exhale slowly.

(Pause)

Be aware of your breathing and visualize the air that comes into and out of in your body... Let these images fill your head for the moment... You simply want to be conscious about your breath... You'd like to become one with the breath... Therefore, you should take every breath is taken... Experience every sensation it triggers... Be aware of your breath as you hold it for a short time within the airways... Then feel the relief when you release that air...

Bring great passion and focus with every breathe you make... Allow your attention and focus on your breathing help you be present in the here and here and now...

Take a deep breath... Take a deep breathe... Then breathe slowly...

Breathe in... Keep your breathe... Then take a deep exhale...

Take a deep breath... Take a deep breathe... Then breathe slowly...

You are now in the present right now... At this moment, all concerns from the past no longer be relevant... At the present, your concerns regarding the future are simple forecasts... These projections really do not really matter...

In the present you're in a space trying to pay attention to you breathing... It is instilling peace and calm inside the you...

You are all you need and your breath... You completeness with your breath is all that is important...

Therefore, take the time to simply be in the moment... Profit of being present and now...

There's no reason to be worried... There is no need to worry... are able to leave your worries behind...

Take a deep breath... Keep your breathe... Then breathe slowly...

Take a deep breath... Take a deep breathe... Then breathe slowly...

Breathe in... Keep your breathing... Then breathe slowly...

(Pause)

Your worries and anxieties are somewhere else... The worries you have don't be a source of stress for you this moment... This is the appeal of being moment... You're present in the moment... In the moment and now is the right time to let go of the tension your body feels...

What are you feeling today? Talk to the physique... You can ask it what it feels like... Do you still feel strain and tension? They should be significantly decreased in the past... It could be located in areas that your muscles feel tight and constricting... The constrictions are as knots... Some are wrapped loosely, but there are others that are tightly... and the tightness is becoming discomforting...

You can then go down and feel your legs and feet... How do they? What are the sensations you can sense in the feet? Are they aching because you had to support your weight when you stood? Are they exhausted due to the motions of walking and moving around? Are the muscles in your legs also aching? Try to take note of the way they feel at the moment. ....

Now, try at rubbing your lower back... Try at noticing your shoulder and neck... There ought to be a bit of tightness in the neck and shoulders as well... You should feel the soreness of your shoulder... It is likely that the discomfort you feel is a result of the load that you carried through all whole day... You should also, feel your back pain... The reason for this is that it was your back that supported you and allowed you to sit straight... The back has been through many times as you worked through every entire day... Then you can feel the stiffness in the neck...

The aches and pains result from your day's work... The discomfort and pain that you are experiencing currently are due to the immense obligation you put on your body's parts... You'll be satisfied with your body's accomplishments... It have been through a difficult day to make sure you could finish your work... so you can accomplish what you set out to accomplish...

Take a moment to take a look at in your mind... Do you notice that you feel like your head is heavy? It could be because of all the worries and concerns... While you were going through your day, it was hard to think of the to come... It was a must that you had to think about this when you thought of brilliant ideas... Also, you required to dig up the memories from previous times... The experiences from the past were filled with crucial knowledge... They also taught you important lessons. important lessons will be crucial when you worked to perfect and enhance your plan...

All these things have caused you to feel a huge amount of anxiety... That's the feeling you're experiencing right currently... the weight of the feeling on your head, and the fatigue that is felt in your entire physique... This is anxiety...

Recall the rhythm of your breath...

Breathe in... Keep your breathe... Then take a deep exhale...

Breathe in... Take a deep breathing... Then breathe slowly...

Take a deep breath... Take a deep breathe... Then breathe slowly...

Relax your breathing and allow your to be in the here and right now... With this, let yourself relax... Relax and let your breathing slash away the walls that the stress has been trying to build...

Breathe in... Take a deep breathing... Then take a deep exhale...

Every inhalation and exhalation gives you the much-needed relief... Then you notice your body's reaction... You'll begin to feel your muscles feel at ease... It's like the knots tightly wound are beginning to loosen... The breath you take is tearing them apart... Inhale more of the joy that your breath can bring...

Take a deep breath... Take a deep breathe... Then take a deep exhale...

Take a deep breath... Keep your breathe... Then take a deep exhale...

Breathe in... Take a deep breathe... Then breathe slowly...

(Pause)

Your body is slowly getting back to rest and recuperating... The time that you've devoted to the present moment are yielding results... The moment you step into the present, you are able to feel your body beginning to ease the tension... You'll feel the tightness in your muscles go away... You'll notice your mind begin to unwind from the burdens and concerns...

As a result you're feeling stressed and anxious. It's about to disappear... As the worries and anxieties had left in the past... Keep up the pace in your breath...

Take a deep breath... Keep your breathe... Then take a deep exhale... As you exhale let stress be a part of it...

Make the most of this opportunity to take a rest... You require this time to recuperate... You'll need this time to free yourself of stress and anxiety...

Forget what happened in the past... Don't think about the future... The things you are thinking about do not exist in the here and today... What is important now is that you're relaxing... Relaxing... anxiety and worries are gradually dissolving...

Breathe in... Take a deep breathing... Then take a deep exhale...

Breathe in... Take a deep breathing... Then breathe slowly...

Take a deep breath... Take a deep breathing... Then take a deep exhale...

Keep bringing in more peace and tranquility within your... When you are ready to come back allow your body to respond to the energy boost that you've just received... Allow your brain to be enthralled by the new freedom it has gained from worries and concerns... Take your time to restore your senses through slow and deliberate motions... Close your eyes once you're fully awake... Take a few minutes to take a step back from your seat. Stress and anxieties are greatly diminished... You are able to take a break and go on with every day full of enthusiasm...

Chapter 11: Hints For How To Study For The First Time

If you've never tried meditation before, it may be difficult to begin from scratch. You might have heard about the luxurious feeling or the extraordinary benefits of relaxation that usually are a result of regular meditation but you're sitting on a couch in your living space wondering what you should do to begin. Is there something you are missing?

Yes, indeed. Like any other beneficial practice, meditation usually requires the practice of. Someone who has been regularly meditating for a long time is more likely to fall into an euphoria state with little or no preparation however, this is the result of self-training. As a novice it's likely that you won't be able to experience the deep relaxation state. It's possible that you won't experience any benefit at all from this practice until you've had a had a few sessions on a regular basis. Here are some guidelines you need to take in mind if you are planning start your meditation journey for the very first time.

Tip#1 1: Set the Scene Tip#1: Setting the Scene

The first step is to locate an area that you'll be doing your workout. It is important to make sure that the area is clean private and private as well as has a pleasant temperature. Make sure that the space you choose is unaffected until the time you complete your practice of meditation. Choose a location that you can relax and not be disturbed. Certain people are able to sit and meditate in the comfort of a chair or couches. But, it is important to make sure that the spot you decide to sit in isn't too comfortable in a way that it makes you feel tired. For those who are just beginning, crosswith your feet on the floor is usually the most suitable option.

The idea of sitting on a cushion is usually suggested if you find that your floor is uncomfortable. Set out a blanket or a towel to keep your feet from becoming cold. Also, dim your lighting and remove any glare that is bright enough to be seen through your eyes closed. One should be able to play music when they like. But, it should be instrumental as the lyrics can be distracting. Also, the music must be quiet. Nature sounds or white noise are perfect.

Tip#2: Getting Yourself Prepared:--

Let yourself loosen up and get comfortable. Be aware in your head that the aim here is to unwind. Get rid of your shoes, loosen your clothes, and do the stretch. As you move in every direction, slowly move your shoulders several times. Then, bend to your hips, and then hang. Then, you can move the arms around and finally tilt your head to the side. Do your best to alleviate any muscle tension that might prevent you from getting the desired results from the exercise. Take care to ease the muscles of your face. The goal to allow every part of your body be relaxed.

Tip#3: Dive In:

Relax in the spot you've prepared and make sure you are comfortable. Don't lean forward, as that can hinder breathing. But, don't push yourself into a rigid, unnatural posture as well. Close your eyes and breathe. Every time you inhale you count one's. You should also count one' every when you exhale. Every breath you take has to be counted as one'. The idea that this is an exercise to strengthen your awareness of the present.

Concentrate on your breath. It should feel like it is inflating the lungs, pressing on the diaphragm and growing your stomach. Be sure to feel how delicious it is inhaling the oxygen-rich air. In general, while you're doing this, your body will slowly begin to relax, and all your attention will definitely be focused on your mind. Be aware it's your very first time to meditate. This is the place you'll must be focused during your subsequent sessions. Now when you've abided by these tips, you'll effortlessly reach your goal.

Tip#4: Coming back:--

Once you're completely settled in your head then it's time to let yourself drift slowly back to the real world. Do a little wiggle with your fingers and toes as you lick your lips and awaken your body gradually. Close your eyes and try to remain in the position for at least 3 minutes as your senses begin to turn to the other direction. Then, slowly get up and you'll be done with your first session.

Chapter 12: Meditations With Guided Voice For Letting Go Of Fear

There are two types of fear: deluded or unhealthy, and healthy or not deluded. They can be further divided in fear of the inexplicable as well as fear of being avoidable. The best way to manage fear is to identify which type of fear we are experiencing and change our unfounded anxieties about what we might not address into solid appropriate fears about what we are able to manage. Then, we'll be able to draw on these fears as motivation to build asylums and beat the things that are very risky and over time, overcome what seems to be inexplicably inevitable, such as like age, disease and death.

Change Fear

When we feel fearful then we should think about what are we really afraid of. Are we able to say that we're scared of getting sick? In any event currently, we have to select between a limited number of options which the fear of becoming sick is not a good thing. It is much more sensible to be fearful of debased resurrection and the 4 streams that are maturing, birth, dying, and death that are all triggered through our dreams. This is an important fear and is referred to as "renunciation" which is the determination to be free from the sufferings of samsara, the motivation that can enable us to liberate ourselves from samsara and all disorder.

Fear of Death

Then again, perhaps we are apprehensive about death. But, again since we're going to be a victim and die, this fear is not useful and could trigger unintentional reactions, like rejection or a feeling of inadequacy or lack of significance in our lives. However, in spite of being aware that you will have to take a step back but we don't have to go out with uncontrollable personality. It's therefore beneficial to transform the fear of passing to a fear of hitting in the dirt with an uncontrollable personality. This is the motivation that ensures peace and a controlled death.

Perhaps it's the fear that people will hate us.

We can change our perception and appreciate them.

Fear of Rejection

Then again, perhaps we fear dismissal. Again, where does this fear actually originate? Perhaps it's the fear of people who hate us. What would we be in a position to change that? Reframe our thinking and become more be like them. This is within our control.

Fear of Being Accused

Our fear of obligation, of being caughtand not having the courage to leave, could transform into a beneficial fear when we recognize that the thing that is the culprit is our personal psychological state. The real and genuine fear stems from the realization that we are not devoted to our escape from samsara and acts as the reason to look for that promise to escape.

Freedom from Fear

In reality, we can't control whether events be in our favor or not, but we can learn the best way to control our personal personalities, our reactions as well as our personal direction, and in this line, we will find certified complete freedom from fear. According to Shantideva in the The Handbook for the Bodhisattva's Life:

The source of all our fears stems from our uncontrollable personalities as well as "dreams".

There are anxieties that arise from connections, for instance anxiety and fear of not being separated from someone or something we think is essential to our security or fulfillment.

There are fears that arise from anger and disdain. Some fears are related to our feelings of being sabotaged by others and that's why we explode, and then try to rationally or physically get rid of the person.

In addition there are anxieties that arise from the psyche of self-realization an understanding of obliviousness which is the basis of all other daydreams and, in this way, the source of all other things.

To overcome this root of fear, Buddha revealed the truth of no self or void.

The Source of All Fear

Self-control can be described as an inability to comprehend the way that things happen and a mind that grasps at us and our surroundings as real, inherently real, existing without the mind and having no connection with our awareness of sight. To conquer this root of all fear Buddha demonstrated the reality of no self or void. This is an important subject but we can improve our understanding by thinking about our dreams.

The same way as an Fantasy

Similar to how all the anxiety or risk that we experience in a bad dream stems from a lack of understanding the reality we're imagining that we are experiencing, then all the fear and endurance we experience throughout our lives stems from not being aware of our world and our experiences. The universe does not exist in isolation from our mind. The idea that everything is "out out there" and are not a part of our mind is the root of our fears. When we realize that everything is predicted by our awareness of the world like the things in a dream, each one of our worries and concerns will go away. We live in the fact that we're asleep or lost in imaginations and will stop experiencing after waking up and see things as they really are. The primary reason for all of Buddha's teachings is to assist us in waking up. get up.

Despite the fact that certain things appear as real, solid and devoid of mental psyche, they're as flawed as a dream.

Let's suppose that last night, we imagined a tiger in pursuit of us. When we imagined it the tiger, it appeared distinctly to be from its own perspective this is why we feared it and retreated away from it. We believed that we were being chased by a real tiger and didn't realize that the tiger was just an representation of our mind. When we finally awake, we realized it was our own projection mind- it was not on its own perspective, inside our tiny room! We quickly figured out our confusion and realized the fact that the animal was our own projection mind so our fears went down.

A Simple Appearance in Mind

The tiger ceased to move at the point that the fantasy psyche had was shut down. The same is true for the world we live in as we sleep. Although it is true that it appears real, authentic and unfettered by the mental psyche, as a practice, it's just as weak as a dream. It is a muddled appearance to mind that appears from the background. It's confusing due to the fact that for the time we're thinking about it, the world of fantasy appears to exist on its own perspective, independent from our mind, whereas in reality, it's simply a mental image. The exact same thing, in every case, holds true for the world we see as we sleep. Even though it is true that the things we see appear real, authentic and devoid of mental psyche, in the end they're as unreal as a dream.

We are completely manipulated by appearances. Not for a second do we doubt their authenticity.

The Sleep of Insanity

All of the things in samsara the body and satisfactions, as well as the universes that we live in are the same as those found in a fairytale. They're all mixed-up appearances that arise from the other unconsciousness. The things that are dishonest appear to exist on their own beyond the psyche and we are completely drawn into their look. If an unpalatable object like the appearance of a foe in our psyche, we believe this image to be real, even if it is not a adversary, and therefore we react by expressing fear or a threat When an attractive item, like an outstanding woman or man is portrayed to us, we too are captivated and feel a sense of envious attachment. We are totally manipulated by the appearance of things - not even ever do we doubt their authenticity. In the event that we were to scrutinize the appearance of things, we'd find that they are: mere appearances to our minds, but with no authentic substance behind them. The enemy we fight or flee from isn't as real as the tiger we encounter in our fantasies and does not have the capacity to alter who we are. Additionally, the wonderful person or woman we're so bonded to looks like a romantic partner that we encounter in a dream or a simple image that appears like a wave within the ocean of our mind before dissolving again further.

How thoughts purge the mind of Fears and Phobias

"Phobia" can be one of many terms that the general population makes use of and misuses. If someone has a fear of something, we say the person has a phobia. however it isn't usually the case. Phobias are an actual mental problem that can negatively affect the lives of individuals; however the fear and weight could be a sound trigger and can lead to accelerate the speed of progress towards risk. Being aware of this potential is the first step to understanding the ways in which reflection can benefit those who suffer from the negative consequences of phobias that are real.

Unease and fear could be a complete waste of time and destroying due to an update that makes your mind is flooded with danger and negative thoughts. If someone was raised in the basement when she was a young tyke such as, for instance it could be that she has an aversion to enclosed areas, or fear of claustrophobia. Even though her fear was rational and justified at the time of the abuse, since her body was trying to get out or fight the dangerous situation the experience is horrifying and thrilling when she arrives in accepting that space is safe when she is an older.

This type of excitement often is a shock to those who experiences it. The heart begins to beat faster as their breathing rate gets greater, and the person could think they are in a state of hyperventilation as memories and silence associated with the actual enhancement flood their mind. The dreadful reaction originates from the amygdala. This is a note framework within the cerebrum, which triggers with the "battle and flight" response. The ideas she is able to formulate about her current condition, being, for instance, "I am apprehensive," are derived from the ventrolateral prefrontal cortex which makes use of words to identify and translate feelings.

The relationship between the amygdala as well as the ventrolateral prefrontal cortex the spot reflection's capability for those who suffer the negative effects of fear. When a person translates their experience into phrases and checks, the activities in her amygdala diminishes. The decrease in the development of the amygdalae reduces or blocks the emotions of freedom for all are typical because of the improvements as well as the belief that they are able to understand how to deliberately process the situation.

Meditation lets you see thoughts and emotions without an emotional response. Concentrate on an affirmative word or an energizing scene within your mind. After you have a moment of silence as an observer of your own mind and body. When new idea or feeling goes through you, you note it , rather than responding to it.

The routine of meditation also prepares your brain to accept the present and present. These fears are rooted in the past and tension is usually due to fear of the near or impossibly distant future. If you focus on the present moment--or are living in the present--your amygdala is able to experience little motivation to take action.

If the person who is claustrophobic was to perform the exercise in a normal way it would be possible to find a way to quickly observe her physical and enthusiastic reactions using words such as "sweat-soaked hands" or "sentiments of fear," and then allow the person to continue by not disorienting their mind. In addition, as they build their ability and desire to focus on the present moment, they increase their ability to stay in the present when they initiate a boost without linking it with a negative previous event.

The continuous routine in relation to contemplation can make you deal with a variety of nonsensical emotions like trepidation and everyday life through the ventrolateral prefrontal cortex which in turn, may slow down or even predict the start of arousing reactions. When a person who is phobic improves her capacity to think , and slowly opens herself up to the subject of her dread and fear, her amygdala will be able to act in the exact manner that is needed.

Meditations to Let Go of Fear

QIGONG MEDITATION

In the traditional Chinese medical practice, it is believed that fear can be put out of the kidneys. In the west we are aware that frightening thoughts are little in comparison to physical and electrical signals which are activated by a perplexing network of connections in the cells of the body. When there is enough redundancy in the system, these neural pathways are organized and consolidated, triggering the same reaction every when a threat is discovered.

The moment the psyche is examined with the possibility of risk, whether it's genuine is the case, or not. It re-visits the same pathways to perform similar things. This is also the point where qigong meditation gets into. When you repeat positive thoughts you will create and strengthen neural pathways and also clear kidneys, assisting you to gain more control over your emotions.

Try it for yourself:

Place your shoulders back and your feet firmly on the floor. Place your hands on your kidneys to the back, under those ribs below. Visualize them and the little adrenal organs that are over them in your mind.

Close your eyes, smile and breathe your stomach. Imagine an ethereal blue glow and a calming harmony surrounding your kidneys and adrenal organs. Breathe out and push your stomach back into.

LEAN IN

The practice of meditation is designed to be common sense, helping us navigate through life with a sense of peace and compassion. Similar to any emotion that comes up, meditation can help calm us in spite of fear to allow us to understand it all more clearly.

The day went on you will be able to face anxiety in a positive way by focusing on the intensity of your meditation.

Do it yourself:

Be sure to check in with your feelings regularly. When you are feeling uncomfortable, let that feeling be.

Instead of running, take a deep breath and reframe your thoughts of fear and anxiety with warmth and awe. Keep your mind on anxiety, just as it would be for your trustworthy companion.

If you're in good shape and space, sit down and breathe to your fears for ten breaths.

Fear as Power

Chris Bertish is a world-record-holding massive wave surfer. Additionally Chris Bertish has some interesting things to say about dread.

"Fear is saying that this is the best moment to make the decision to achieve what you're trying to achieve. Your body is making you ready for the desired outcome. If you are able to comprehend that fear is similar to other feelings it is possible to figure out how to control it. After that you'll be able perform actions that majority of people think are unusual."

Bertish has discovered how to control and manage his fear in a way that works for him, allowing it to assist him in achieving amazing feats of unison.

Try it for yourself:

To overcome the fear that I have of climbing I've conquered my anxiety by taking a lead rock climbing course where I have to climb up towards the highest point of the divider. I then free fall down the divider , before being securely secured by rope.

Through the process of training, receptiveness as well as cheering my teachers and friends I've learned how to breathe through the fear and release it repeatedly. However, the fear is still there, but my reaction toward it has evolved.

Have you tried it out yourself? -- What's your biggest fear? What simple, safe steps can you use to rid yourself of your breath in the worry? When you are practicing the technique, what are the changes you notice after a while?

A Simple Visualization

It is possible to try this basic thought process to release anxiety and fear. In a comfortable position to contemplate, and sitting straight, shut our eyes and breathe normally through our noses. Then we put in a bit of time identifying what we're currently scared of. We identify our manipulated unwanted fears such as fears of being passed it on or causing misfortune or disappointment or disappointment, etc. By using our brains we can see that each single one of those fears along with any other threats, are a result of because of our betrayed personality and our antagonistic actions.

It is then possible to recognize the fears as one the causes that they stem from, personality negative, and their actions in the form of a dense cloud of smoke when the exhale. The bad smoke dissipates and disappears. When you breathe and imagine that you're absorbing all the excitement and vitality made up of white light. This light is a source of energy for our mind and body.

After doing this for after a couple of times, we start to feel that our body and brain become totally free. We have received everything we wanted and feel safe and blessed in the company of others. We can feel our body becoming soft and supple, with a clear peaceful, confident, and calm mind.

Let the sensation gradually disperse from your body and let it overflow your entire body and body.

Give thanks for the support you received during a tough period.

Remember that we have a free decision. Soul sees us through and through freedom, therefore we must seek help whenever needed.

When you're experiencing anxiety or fear ensure that you practice this thought. After a while your worries are likely to become less and more rational however, it takes effort and repetition.

Chapter 13: The Light Warrior Meditation

This third practice blends with the Body Scan meditation and the Meditation of the Sun to give you a profound feeling of relaxation and helping you to relax and relieve anxiety.

I've employed this technique throughout the most challenging times of my life, and it helped me get back to the top of my game. This is why it holds an important place in my heart, and that is why I chose to share the method within this book. I truly hope that everyone can profit from this book.

The first step is to begin the meditation with a long body scan as described in the first method in the book. It is important to take time to complete the process in a proper manner, since it is the grounding part and is crucial to the whole practice.

Then, we'll take a few minutes to perform the exercise with liquid sunlight because it gives us the capability to melt stress and anxiety off our bodies.

In the end, we'll direct our attention to positive and loving thoughts, which will serve as our guiding principles for the rest throughout the entire day. The positive outlook will always bring positive energy into our lives, which is the reason why you will see that the Light Warrior goes through life with positive vibes and good goals: he realizes that the world mirrors his and will return what he contributes to the world.

Let's get started!

Find a comfortable, calm and in a balanced and comfortable place. You can fully be present with yourself and let your body and your mind settle down until they are comfortable and calm.

Breathe in, relax...

Breathe out, relax...

Breathe in and relax...

Breathe out, relax...

Breathe in, relax...

Take a deep breath, be calm...

Breathe in and relax...

Breathe out, relax...

Let your mind disengage from all thoughts and concentrate to your breath. Relax and breathe naturally. Don't insist on a specific rhythm. Breathe in and let it let it go.

Take care, now, to shift your focus away from breath to the space where you are.

Feel the atmosphere and energy of this place throughout your being. Be aware of the sounds that are on the other side. Perhaps there's a clock running, or perhaps cars are passing right outside your window. Whatever it is, it's okay, just let your focus remain focused on the outside.

Breathe in, relax...

Take a deep breath, be calm...

Breathe in, relax...

Breathe out, relax...

Breathe in, relax...

Breathe out, relax...

Breathe in, relax...

Take a deep breath, be calm...

Bring your focus back to the breath. Be patient and you'll soon find a feeling of comfort and relaxation. Keep this relaxed state in which you can feel your body and mind at peace, calm and at peace for a short time, and not letting your attention wander on your breathing.

Breathe in, relax...

Breathe out, relax...

Breathe in, relax...

Breathe out, relax...

Breathe in, relax...

Take a deep breath, be calm...

Breathe in, relax...

Breathe out, relax...

Breathe in, relax...

Take a deep breath, be calm...

Breathe in, relax...

Take a deep breath, be calm...

Breathe in and relax...

Breathe out, relax...

Breathe in, relax...

Breathe out, relax...

Begin to look around your body starting from your feet toward high above your head. Take your time and then stop at each area of your body and be attentive to what it has to say. If you are feeling tight on an area, hold your attention on the area until you feel that it is relaxing. It is essential to not overdo the process. Just breathe and you will notice your body becoming increasingly relaxed.

Start with your biggest toes. How do they feel now? Have you ever thought about this question? Imagine a clear image of them in your head while you shift your attention towards your ankles.

In this exercise, every joint can be a key location where anxiety could be absorbed. If you spot a portion of your body that is tight, you can gently massage it using your fingers until at ease.

Breathe in, relax...

Take a deep breath, be calm...

Breathe in, relax...

Breathe out, relax...

Breathe in and relax...

Take a deep breath, be calm...

Breathe in and relax...

Breathe out, relax...

Take your knees to your chest and feel the knees. What are your knees like today? Perhaps they're aching due to sitting all day long or put in efforts yesterday. Perhaps they're calm and sturdy. Whatever it is good, you're in the right place. By extending your quadriceps up to your pelvic floor and the genital region.

It is a crucial part of your body that is crucial in the case of stress and anxiety, since much of your energy is channeled to it through the neuromuscular system.

Take a few minutes to focus on your pelvic area before moving up. I'll give you the time you require.

Breathe in and relax...

Take a deep breath, be calm...

Breathe in and relax...

Take a deep breath, be calm...

Breathe in, relax...

Take a deep breath, be calm...

Breathe in, relax...

Take a deep breath, be calm...

Breathe in, relax...

Breathe out, relax...

Breathe in, relax...

Take a deep breath, be calm...

Breathe in and relax...

Breathe out, relax...

Breathe in, relax...

Breathe out, relax...

Breathe in, relax...

Take a deep breath, be calm...

Breathe in and relax...

Take a deep breath, be calm...

Breathe in and relax...

Take a deep breath, be calm...

Breathe in and relax...

Breathe out, relax...

Continue going upwards by extending your chest and your shoulders. This is where lots of tension is discovered, so you should be patient in this region. If you are feeling a little stiff, don't be afraid in moving your arms until they are in an appropriate posture. Check your heart and lungs remain strong, regardless of having an unpleasant day or are experiencing problems at present.

The heart continues to beat and breathing, while the lungs continue to breathe.

Breathe in, relax...

Take a deep breath, be calm...

Breathe in, relax...

Take a deep breath, be calm...

Breathe in and relax...

Take a deep breath, be calm...

Breathe in, relax...

Breathe out, relax...

Breathe in, relax...

Take a deep breath, be calm...

Breathe in, relax...

Breathe out, relax...

Breathe in, relax...

Breathe out, relax...

Breathe in, relax...

Take a deep breath, be calm...

Then you finally reach your head. Continue to breathe deeply in your head, and you can feel the air filling every empty space on your head.

What is the feeling of the air? Are you feeling warm or cold? What scent does it have? Are you a fan? These are the simple questions we don't ask ourselves throughout the day. However, they can help us get and return to our body.

Breathe in and relax...

Take a deep breath, be calm...

Breathe in and relax...

Take a deep breath, be calm...

Breathe in, relax...

Take a deep breath, be calm...

Breathe in and relax...

Breathe out, relax...

Enjoy this wonderful area for the time you like and you're worthy of it.

Breathe in, relax...

Take a deep breath, be calm...

Breathe in, relax...

Breathe out, relax...

Breathe in and relax...

Breathe out, relax...

Breathe in and relax...

Take a deep breath, be calm...

Breathe in, relax...

Breathe out, relax...

Breathe in and relax...

Take a deep breath, be calm...

Breathe in, relax...

Take a deep breath, be calm...

Breathe in and relax...

Take a deep breath, be calm...

Breathe in, relax...

Breathe out, relax...

Breathe in, relax...

Breathe out, relax...

Breathe in, relax...

Take a deep breath, be calm...

Breathe in and relax...

Breathe out, relax...

Breathe in, relax...

Breathe out, relax...

Breathe in and relax...

Breathe in, relax...

Take a deep breath, be calm...

Breathe in, relax...

Breathe out, relax...

Then bring your focus back to your body, and begin feeling your legs and arms again. It is possible to close your arms or move them in order to control the space surrounding you.

Keep your eyes shut for a while and just enjoy the moment that you live in. You've given yourself time to heal and that's amazing.

Breathe in, relax...

Breathe out, relax...

Breathe in, relax...

Take a deep breath, be calm...

Breathe in, relax...

Take a deep breath, be calm...

Breathe in and relax...

Breathe out, relax...

When you have time you can try to imagine the sphere of sunlight just a few inches higher than your head. Imagine a tiny sun could be helpful during this time since it assists your body and mind adjust to the new reality.

Every breath you take now take a moment to feel the light flowing down your neck and your spine. getting to the bottom of your feet via the pelvic floor as well as your legs. Your body is filled with this soft and warm gentle light. Are you feeling it?

If you're having trouble with it, don't worry but don't force it to much. It will improve with time.

Breathe in and relax...

Take a deep breath, be calm...

Breathe in, relax...

Breathe out, relax...

Breathe in and relax...

Breathe out, relax...

Breathe in, relax...

Breathe out, relax...

Breathe in, relax...

Take a deep breath, be calm...

Breathe in, relax...

Take a deep breath, be calm...

Breathe in and relax...

Breathe out, relax...

Breathe in and relax...

Take a deep breath, be calm...

The sunshine is taking over every inch of your body and rid of all the stress and tension from your day. Relax, I'll allow you to stay for a few minutes to be in this state of bliss as the sun's light is cleansing your soul and body.

Breathe in, relax...

Take a deep breath, be calm...

Breathe in, relax...

Take a deep breath, be calm...

Breathe in, relax...

Breathe out, relax...

Breathe in and relax...

Take a deep breath, be calm...

Breathe in and relax...

Breathe out, relax...

Breathe in and relax...

Breathe out, relax...

Breathe in and relax...

Take a deep breath, be calm...

Breathe in, relax...

Breathe out, relax...

Breathe in, relax...

Breathe out, relax...

Breathe in and relax...

Breathe out, relax...

Breathe in, relax...

Take a deep breath, be calm...

Breathe in, relax...

Take a deep breath, be calm...

Breathe in and relax...

Breathe out, relax...

Breathe in, relax...

Take a deep breath, be calm...

Breathe in and relax...

Breathe out, relax...

Breathe in, relax...

Breathe out, relax...

When the light falls down your body, you can feel your body filling up not just with warm liquid but also with positive and loving thoughts , too.

Pay attention to everything positive that's happening throughout the world. The fact that you're still breathing and alive is an amazing feat that is all it takes, so take note of it in your head. Visualize something that makes you feel happy and that is a reflection of positive energy within your life.

Personally, I prefer to imagine a gorgeous blooming white rose, however you are able to select whatever suits your heart most. Simply paint the image in your mind and breathe it in.

Breathe in, relax...

Take a deep breath, be calm...

Breathe in and relax...

Take a deep breath, be calm...

Breathe in and relax...

Take a deep breath, be calm...

Breathe in, relax...

Breathe out, relax...

Clear and clear images are important, because it allows you to carry it around for the rest of the day. This is why I'll offer you the entire time you require.

Breathe in and relax...

Take a deep breath, be calm...

Breathe in, relax...

Take a deep breath, be calm...

Breathe in and relax...

Take a deep breath, be calm...

Breathe in, relax...

Breathe out, relax...

Breathe in, relax...

Take a deep breath, be calm...

Breathe in and relax...

Take a deep breath, be calm...

Breathe in, relax...

Breathe out, relax...

Breathe in, relax...

Breathe out, relax...

Breathe in, relax...

Take a deep breath, be calm...

Breathe in, relax...

Breathe out, relax...

Breathe in, relax...

Take a deep breath, be calm...

Breathe in, relax...

Breathe out, relax...

Then bring your focus back to your body, and begin feeling your legs and arms again. You can either close the fingers or open them to be in control of the space surrounding you.

Keep your eyes shut for a while and just enjoy the moment you're living. You've allowed yourself time to be better, and that's a huge accomplishment.

Breathe in and relax...

Take a deep breath, be calm...

Breathe in and relax...

Take a deep breath, be calm...

Breathe in, relax...

Take a deep breath, be calm...

Breathe in, relax...

Breathe out, relax...

Then, become aware of the surroundings surrounding you. Be aware of the sounds that surround you as well as temperatures of the space you are in , and when you're ready, you can you can open your eyes once more.

Chapter 14: Dedicating Your Efforts
Figure 7 Free Credits

Once you've finished your meditation practice Now is the time to focus on other tasks. You need to establish the connections that we make between the actions we do every day. This is done in order to recognize the effects of sound that meditation gives us on a regular basis. If we practice this, we become motivated by the practices of meditation we're practicing. This means that we be able to keep going at it for as long as we can to take care of our bodies. If you're prone to conclude your meditation and proceed to other tasks without taking some time to reflect the things you were doing your meditation, the exercises will have little effect. It will not be a full experience of nutrition the way you ought to. Imagine a snowflake falling upon hot stones. One of the best methods that you can ensure that you are getting all the benefits from these meditation exercises is to be committed. If you are committed you'll gain positive energy that can serve your life for a long time, and the nourishment you receive from all aspects of your life will be longer. This way, you'll also be able to reach your meditation goals, and their effects will last as long as the ocean or the sky.

Merit Dedication

When you begin your daily meditation routine it is important to set an ideal and a plan of what you wish to achieve through this meditation. Consider, for instance, that the exercises you do will be infused with positive energy that influences your past, future as well as your present. Think about how this positive energy you've generated by meditative practice can help you eliminate negative things. These could be natural disasters that occur or the pain you've experienced during the course of your life. Other examples are injustices that you have that you have faced, such as crimes, war, and the famine. Imagine that all negative events that could happen in the future . They will be removed by the positive energy you've collected. Imagine that you've developed a strength that can eliminate mental and physical illnesses that can affect your life.

Consider that you want the life you live to be filled with excitement, joy as well as zeal and enthusiasm by the power you have created through meditation and keeping your commitment to succeed.

Do not think of meditation as if you are able to take a huge slice of cake. However, if you share it with a huge group with a large number of others, the only chance is that every person will get only a small portion. The principle behind the practice of meditation means that each person is given the entire cake. Additionally, with this power you've created, you can wish for positive things for humanity in general and imagine them all having a good life and not suffering discomfort and suffering. Imagine those with hate, greed, insanity and other negative qualities are free of these vices to enable them to attain the ideal characteristics that humans should possess. The goal is to ensure that they are educated to become god-like beings who are able to live their lives fully. If you practice this devotion your energy achieved during the meditation can lead to positive results.

Chapter 15: Breathing For Relaxation

Breathing to relax is an integral component of meditation guided, and is something that many people don't know is a skill that is beneficial that you can use to help you relax effectively. What is it that's special about breathing? How do you do it? So, keep reading to learn more.

Breathe!

The most likely thing you've heard that relaxing that you should breathe in or even take some deep breaths. This advice is usually given when we're stressed or worried. You may be wondering why you're told this when you're feeling upset and stressed however it's actually helpful when you're anxious and can change the speed at which you respond to the body's breathing as well as anxiety. Diaphragmic breathe is an breathing method which is quite effective. It creates a sensation that communicates to the brain the idea of security.

I wouldn't recommend using this at the moment you're stressed out however, you must in the event of an unsettling situation, apply this technique to make the right decision when trying to determine what you should do next.

Additionally, breathing is beneficial for relaxing and is an essential aspect of relaxing your body while trying to reduce stress. Breathing during a long, stressful day can be very emotional, and it's something that many people don't realize they don't practice.

It is vital to breathe in meditation as are couple of methods to effectively breathe in an meditative state We'll teach you how here.

Diaphragmic Breathing

Also referred to as Eupnea (also known as belly breathing), this is an breathing technique that aids to strengthen the diaphragm. Learning to breathe through your diaphragm can be beneficial since it can help ease the body, breathing, and so on. A lot of the time we don't actually breathe with our diaphragms which results in breaths that are shorter that don't provide oxygen-rich air into the body. It results in taking breaths that do not help to in calming the body and they don't provide a refreshing experience. It's a good thing that you can learn to breathe using your diaphragm and we'll show you how to do it here.

When you're breathing for meditation, using your diaphragm it is best to sit with your feet on the ground or lying down. Set your hands over your stomach. Then close your eyes and begin breathing slow and in a relaxed manner. The belly should be filled by taking a regular breath but don't over-breath. Your hands will move as you breathe like you're filling the balloon. Don't raise your shoulders when you breathe in. Instead concentrate on breathing in your stomach.

When you are at this stage, exhale in a count of five. Reduce the speed of exhaling. After exhaling, hold the breath for a few seconds before breathing this into the air once more. Keep working to maintain the speed and slowness of breathing that you are doing present. Repeat this for 10 or so minutes and repeat this daily for 10 minutes every time. Perform this daily routine to assist you in your private meditation.

You can combine this with the breath, and if you are confronted by an unsettling thought it is possible to remove that thought by acknowledging it and then just letting it remain until it's gone, but not focusing about it. However, if this is too difficult for you, spend some time and concentrate on learning how to breathe in a healthy way. It's a crucial aspect of understanding how to breathe through the diaphragm, and is crucial.

A couple of tips to learn from the exercise are. It is important to focus on the speed of your breathing rather than the intensity of your breath. Do not sneeze through taking more deep breaths, instead keep it slow and steady.

Be aware that you're not going to be able instantly stop anxiety. This isn't how it is done, but instead, breathing can assist you in learning how to relax and be able to get through an even more difficult situation. it can be used as a way to practice breathing more calmly as time goes on.

Do not be afraid to try this as well. It is a lengthy process for mastery, however it can greatly assist.

4-7-8 breath

4-7-8 breathing can be compared to the breathing technique of breathing out your diaphragm however it is a bit of a more a timed exercise. It is beneficial for those suffering from insomnia or anxiety as it assists your body and mind to focus on your breathing instead of thinking about your worries.

How to begin is to lay down or sit, with your hand resting on your stomach, while keeping the other one on your chest, just like how you breathe out of your diaphragm. What you should do is, when you breathe in slowly, you take slow deep breaths that travel straight to your belly then, you silently count to four each time you breathe into your belly.

In this stage when you are not exhaling immediately and then counting silently from 1 until 7. When you reach 7, you exhale fully, and then count in a continuous manner from 1 until 8, removing all oxygen out of lung. You should try to flush all air out by the time you've reached eight. Once you've reached eight, will repeat this until you are completely relaxed. In this case I would suggest that writing down how you are feeling at conclusion of the exercise, as well as what you feel. You're likely be feeling more calm than before. This is especially beneficial when you're in a position where you have to focus on numbers, and if you happen to be someone who requires a sense of groundedness I recommend this.

Equal Breathing

Sama Vritti is like the numbered breathing that has been proven to reduce stress and maintain your relaxed as it balances your mind. At first with, breathe in for four times and then exhale for four counts. It is important to ensure that your breathing occurs through your nose. This is because it builds an inherent resistance as you breathe.

It is a basic pranayama that is a kind of breathing that is meditative, and this technique is employed in a variety of instances in yoga, too. Many people prefer to intensify the rate of breathing to six or more counts or even eight, with the aim of relaxing nerves, increasing concentration on their breathing, and feeling the tension disappear from your body. The greatest benefit of doing this is the fact that it could perform well prior to sleeping, and if you're feeling anxious just before getting ready to go to sleep you can use this technique to reduce distracting thoughts.

Alternate Breathing in the Nostril

Nadi Shodhana is breathing method that assists people suffering from anxiety. It is a sophisticated breathing technique that is great to relax as it clears your mind and calms your body and emotions. This method is extremely effective and helps you balance your body, relax, and activate both sides of your brain. What you should begin is to be in an upright or lying down place, then take your right thumband place it in one nostril on the left. Inhale in, however, make sure to breathe in only through the left nostril. When you are inhaling at the peak you should close the left nostril by closing it with your finger that you are holding at this point. After that take a breath out of on the other side. It's more challenging than you might think however, it requires some coordination. You are able to continue doing this by breathing through the right side while exhaling out the left.

This is a fantastic option for those times when you're stressed out and you're in need of to get your energy flowing and concentrate. Do not do this before going to bed as it won't allow you to relax however, it will to remove the stress from the negative areas of your body, and allow you to concentrate more. So, if you're trying to get your energy back prior to going through stressful situations This is a good option to give it a go.

Skull Shining Breath

Also known as kapalbhati is an internal cleansing process that helps eliminate the toxins that are within your body. It helps cleanse, rejuvenate and rejuvenate your body However, this is one of the most complicated kinds of breathing techniques. What you do is to begin with an exhale that's very long and also slow followed by following it up with a powerful exhale, which you generate. Once you're confident with your contraction you'll want to breathe in and out through your nose for around 2 to 3 seconds, for about

10 seconds total. This is the best way to awaken the body and eliminate the negative emotions. Although it won't provide you with a lot of benefits in terms of overall relaxation, it's an extremely important form of breathing because it's a fantastic way to unwind your body from thoughts that are stressful and allow you to be in a more centered state of mind, which will it will allow you to gain a clear understanding of the things you have to do in your day. It's also a good option to use if you're struggling with lots of worries within your mind and you're looking to let them go. This is a more advanced method and I would suggest to wait until you're prepared.

Conclusion

We've all heard about how reflection can lead to more vivid mental clarity as well as lower levels of stress and a decrease in anxiety. But, how can contemplation help the mind? Research has shown that practicing care causes positive physiological changes that enhance the connection between contemplation and the cerebrum, progressively important.

In the last few decades the practice of contemplation has come to be more common. People are putting their energy into engaging their minds and breathing and learning how to embrace the energy of the present moment. The idea of reflection gatherings is popping everywhere - in networks, schools seniors' focuses, and in the in the past. The trend is being so widespread that the business community has joined the trend of reflection. There's even evidence to show that it can improve your mind.

The field of brain science confirmed what all meditators know that contemplation is beneficial to the body as well as the soul. Scientists are currently preparing to support these claims by showing how contemplation physical influences the incredibly insecure organ that lies between our ears. The ongoing logical evidence supports that reflection supports the components of the cerebrum that contribute to the prosperity. It is also evident that the practice of observing a customary one is to deprive the pressure and unease related parts from the cerebrum the nutrients they require.

Stress is among the most debilitating emotions you can experience. Stress is a mental approach that helps people develop the skills to manage stress and anxiety. Not just emotional stress, but various situations that can result in physical health issues both in the in the short and long term.

The sad thing is that stress is that it's not always so stressful as stress itself, even though it can be very uncomfortable to the person who is anxious, but it is the fear of the reactions of others is a reason for them to trust the person they trust, whether it is a family member, friend or even a coworker, or even experts of managing stress.

Equally we are all aware of the consequences that stress can bring and if you are reading this book for an answer or even relief from stress or an adored one, the results of stress do not require an explanation.

Based on what you've the knowledge, tackling stress begins by identifying the causes of stress that you have for your life. It's not as easy as it seems. The real benefits of your strain aren't always obvious and it's easy to forget your thoughts, feelings, and even your strain-related behaviors.

Another fact that is sad about the management of stress, and having been an anger and stress management expert myself and knowing this thoroughly, is that there's a common assumption that stress management isn't important. This is an "spongy" idea that isn't necessary or is only intended for weak people.

The management of stress is crucial and overcoming anxiety is essential to be successful at work and to lead a happy life.

Sometimes life can be a extremely stressful time. We all have moments when we fear that depression and anxiety will swallow our whole. If you've experienced this feeling it is important to realize that you're not the only one in this feeling.

If this is not your first time you've tried meditation, I hope this small book has convinced you to this intriguing and ever-changing world.

To your success!

www.ingramcontent.com/pod-product-compliance
Lightning Source LLC
Chambersburg PA
CBHW071837080526
44589CB00012B/1031